Narrative Leadership:

Leading with Elegance, Efficiency, and Efficacy

Rabbi Rob Abramovitz M.Div, MBA

L:E&D™
Leadership: Education & Development

www.NarrativeLead.com

SACRED CIRCLE PRESS
Portland, Oregon

Copyright © 2014 by Rob Abramovitz

Published by Sacred Circle Press
Portland, Oregon

All rights reserved. No part of this publication may be reproduced, stored in a retrieval system, or transmitted, in any form or by any means, electronic, mechanical, photocopying, recording, or otherwise, without the prior permission of the author.

ISBN: 0-9763350-6-9

Acknowledgments

Many thanks to my wife, Carolyn, and the great faculty, staff, and students at Marylhurst University.

Table of Contents

Elevators, Guns and the Art of Leadership 1
How to Read This Book 3
    Organization of This Book 3
    Notations 4
    This Book as a Narrative 5
Introduction to Narrative Leadership 7
    What Is Narrative Leadership? 7
    What Is a Narrative Leader? 10
    Roots of Narrative Leadership 12
    Narratives & Stories 15
    Narratives & Memes 17
    Expressed & Foundational Narratives 18
    Leader vs Manager 20
    Foundational Narratives 44
    Narratives & Internal Politics 46
    Leadership Narratives 49
    Cross-Cultural Leadership 61
    Management Narratives 64
    Executive Narratives 69
    Narrative Leadership Examples 71
Ethics & Leadership 75
    Several Quick Example 75
    Trust & Leadership 77
    Respect & Leadership 84
    Know What You Don't Know 85
    The Narrative of Ethics 88
    Elements of Leadership 90
Discovering Foundational Narratives 91
    Using Contextual Clues 91
    Communication Level 95
    Assumptive Words 96
    Rose-Colored Glasses 98
Leadership Styles 101

    Authoritarian Leader 103
    Bossy-Boss 107
    Drama King/Queen 109
    Expert 110
    Fear-Based Leadership... 112
    His/Her Highness 115
    Know-It-All 116
    Laissez-Faire Management 117
    Loner 120
    Micromanager 121
    Narcissistic Leadership... 122
    Nerd 125
    NO! Leader 126
    Out-Of-Integrity Leader 128
    Peer Leader 130
    Narrative Leader 132

Startups - The Beginning of It All 135
    A Short, True Story 136
    The Narratives of Startups 137
    Passion & Narratives 138
    Startups, Creativity, & Groupthink 140
    Mission Statements & Knowing Who You Are 142
    Catchphrases 143
    Hiring for Startups and Young Organizations 144

Selecting a Team 149
    Five Step Hiring Process 149
    Creating an Environment That Works 153

Metrics 159
    Types of Metrics 159
    Measuring Foundational Narratives (Surprises) 161
    Measuring The Work Environment for Innovation (Sparks) 164
    Measuring Implicit Leadership (Golden Glow) 167

What's Next? 171
    Why Start With Metrics? 171

Appendices **175**
   Mental Health Resources 175
   Surprises & Sparks Worksheet...177
   Glossary 178

Table of Figures

Figure 1: Home Page of Website: www.NarrativeLead.com 30
Figure 2: Blackberry's Bottom-Line with Sales & Market Share...42
Figure 3: Ease of Changing the Different Types of Narratives 45
Figure 4: Pew Research on Trust 78
Figure 5: Ethical Values Scale 89
Figure 6: Surprises & Sparks Example 163

I. Elevators, Guns and the Art of Leadership

The elevator doors opened and out rushed two pale and tense corporate executives. They grabbed my arms and pulled me into an empty office. "One of your guys is coming back with a gun. He's going to kill us all!"

True story.

How do we lead/manage when someone has gone out for a gun... or even when we are bored silly sitting in another non-productive meeting? Leaders deal with a whole range of situations, while trying to bring out the best in everyone. How do we even know what is the "best" for everyone?

Narrative Leadership is a process with a structure for gaining deep insight into the chaotic world of leadership. Narrative Leadership delineates the areas that need attention and describes what to do about them. It also offers a concrete measurement system for near real-time gauging of a manager's leadership ability.

Leadership and management are an art.

Narrative Leadership is an essential tool in that art.

[For more on the "elevator and gun" story see the section "Leader vs Manager," page 20."]

II. How to Read This Book

All of the examples used in this book are real. The situations have not been modified to make my point.

This book is designed to be read in short spurts. Each section can be read in under 10 minutes. Also, this book need not be read in a linear fashion, although there are a few "Read Me First" sections. If you're one of those people who like to skip around or just select out the parts in which you are most interested. Here are the sections that should be read first:

- "Introduction to Narrative Leadership," page 7 through "What Is a Narrative Leader?," page 10.
- "Expressed & Foundational Narratives," page 18 through "Explicit & Implicit Leadership," page 27.
- "Foundational Narratives," page 44.
- "Ethics & Leadership," page 75 through "Respect & Leadership," page 84.

Organization of This Book

This first chapter is about the basic structure of the book itself. It's only a few pages, so please read on. Reading this chapter will help speed your understanding within the rest of the book. Chapter 2 is an overview of Narrative Leadership. It's sprinkled with real life examples to help the reader have a deeper understanding of the many definitions that are specific to Narrative Leadership. It's helpful to have words that mean very specific things so that when leaders get together and talk about specific issues the language of Narrative Leadership assists them in describing and understanding the issues at hand.

Chapter 3 describes ethics in narrative terms and begins a move towards the measurement of ethics against a standardized yardstick. Chapter 4 gets into the heart of Narrative Leadership. With the understandings developed in the previous chapter, chapter 5 analyzes sixteen common leadership styles. Chapter 6 looks at leadership styles and their effect upon startups and other young organizations. Chapter 7 is about hiring, firing, and developing a team. Chapter 8 is another foundational chapter. It deals with how to measure leadership. Chapter 9 is about looking forward both for the reader and for me, the writer. In the appendices is a glossary listing all the definitions given throughout the book and a set of resources that may assist Narrative Leaders.

Notations

The names used are all pseudonyms. I have created a naming system to guide you in distinguishing people's roles within the organizational setting. Personal names beginning with "C" relate to someone in the executive suite.

> **C-suite**: *The executives of an organization. So called because most of the members have "C" for "Chief" in their title (e.g. Chief Executive Officer, Chief Technology Officer, etc.).*

If a person is a manager, the name used will begin with "M." If their main role in the discussion is as a founder of the organization, the name used will begin with "F." An "E" is used if the name relates to an employee/worker level person. For example Charlie and Charlene would both be in the C-suite, Mark and Mary are managers, Fred and Flora are founders, and Eric and Evelyn are employees.

Definitions are indented, in *slightly larger, italicized type*. The word being defined is given in **bold**. Definitions are given in the glossary as well as in the text.

Comments that are pithy summaries are also in *slightly larger, italicized type*, but no part is bolded.

In the Appendix is a glossary of all the terms used in this book. One of the purposes of this book is to develop a vocabulary for Narrative Leadership. Leaders can think clearly about their work with appropriate terms to describe what they are seeing, feeling, and hearing.

Gender issues: English has no pronoun (e.g. "he" and "she") that includes both genders. Therefore, I have tended to switch back and forth between genders every section. My purpose is to engage people of all genders. Even though our personal narratives are modified by our maleness or femaleness, the overarching Narrative Leadership model applies equally regardless of gender.

This Book as a Narrative

Since this book is about narrative, it is written in a narrative style. Sometimes it will follow a thought into a side-issue. These side-issues would be sections in themselves in a standard, linearly organized text. But these side issues help illuminate the story at the point they are injected. Most texts would have chapters upon chapters of preparation work before getting to the essence. Here, I have interwoven the explanatory details with the examples. Note that I have written this book in the first person; it is written from me specifically for you. That is, this book is a narrative, of which I am the narrator.

Narratives are informed by the experiences of the narrator. My experiences have mostly been in high technology business. I have also consulted with, worked for, and been on the boards of many nonprofits and worked for much of a decade in low technology business. My experience is that Narrative Leadership works well in all venues requiring leaders. My terminology, though, is oriented towards high-tech. My hope is that you can translate this in a way that informs your own leadership style.

This book is not a "how-to" management book. This book is meant to assist leaders in understanding their world as well as the understanding and management of change.

III. Introduction to Narrative Leadership

What if you, as a leader, knew where best to put your time and energy, knew when you had made a good decision, and knew where problems were going to occur before they happened? What if you were able to bring out the best in people and were able to measurably improve the organization for which you work?

Narrative Leadership (NL) directly addresses these issues and brings leadership technology into the 21st century.

What Is Narrative Leadership?

Many years ago, I was asked to manage a small group. Because I had the right college degree (oceanography), the company thought that I would be able to appropriately manage this group. The people I was assigned to lead were older and more experienced than I. They had fun playing with their new manager. Fortunately, most of the time I could laugh at my own lack of management skill.

It wasn't youth that hindered me from achieving my goal of being a good manager; it was something much more fundamental. I didn't understand the context of management. I had read books about management, watched TV and movies that had actors playing at management, and thought about how great a manager I would be - but I had no understanding of the management gestalt.

> ***Management gestalt***: *The entirety of what it takes to be a good manager. The form and substance of a manager. "Gestalt" is from the German, meaning "form" or "shape."*

Over the years, I kept looking for the key to what makes a good manager. I read books, got more university degrees, and tried different approaches. After many years, I finally concluded that we, as a society, don't really know what makes good management.

Society looks at the current profitability of a business and equates that with excellence in management.

The problem with using profitability as the measurement of good management is that it is highly complex and is ancient data. Firstly, there were a myriad of small management decisions that resulted in the organizational profitability. And secondly, the factors that went into making last quarter's profits came from management decisions made long ago. Some of the managers who made those decisions aren't with the company any longer!

As an executive hiring managers, my problem became much more than a personal quest for excellence. My problem became fourfold:

- how to recognize good managers
- how to learn from, expand upon, and train people in good leadership practices
- how to measure good management
- how to know when managers had made a good decision (in near-real-time).

Narrative Leadership directly addresses all four of these questions. Narrative Leadership is a methodology for understanding what makes good management, a model for good management, and a system of quality measurement for management. And it all starts with story.

Humans understand the universe through stories. We tell ourselves a story of who we are and how we fit into (or don't fit into) our society. We have a story of what our society is and how we relate to our friends. We use story to make sense out of a complex world. We are besieged by data. In order to make sense of this barrage of data, we make up a story of what is important and what is not.

We use words as components to make up these stories, but every word has a story behind it that we learned. For example, every adult has a huge story about their name. This "name-story" extends over decades in time, and miles and miles of space.

Our understanding of the words "company," "work," "employee," "leader," and "manager" are all complex stories that change with our experiences. Narrative Leadership gives us a framework for understanding this chaotic storm of information and narratives.

> ***Narrative Leadership (NL)****: A model for guiding organizations and people towards excellence by the directed use of story.*

Let's break down this definition. A model is an abstraction of reality that explains a portion of reality. An individual's story (singular, but ever changing) of the outside world is a model. Most management books are about tools rather than models. A tool is a means of accomplishing a task. Semi-famous management tools include: "The One Minute Manager" (Kenneth Blanchard), "The Ideal Executive" (Ichak Adizes), and "The 7 Habits of Highly Successful People" (Stephen Covey). These are all tools. None are models of reality that explain leadership. Narrative Leadership is a model.

A good leader not only knows where she is going but also, how to get there, how to know when she is off the track, what to do when she gets off track, and how to make it enjoyable for all the people she is leading. These elements are all part of NL.

I like wikipedia's definition of excellence:

> ***Excellence****: A talent or quality which is unusually good and surpasses ordinary standards.*

This definition incorporates the principle of a standard against which results can be measured. This measure can be used to determine how good a leader actually is. Metrics are an integral part of NL. In fact, NL is designed so that the use of metrics alone, starts the leader as well as the rest of the organization down the road of Narrative Leadership. NL metrics are designed to act like a virus that spreads excellence and the understanding of story throughout an organization.

> ***Metric****: A measure against some type of ruler.*

Narrative Leadership Metric: A measure of the stories involved and how they drive the person or organization towards excellence.

From now on, when I refer to "metric," I will be referring to the NL metric.

Metrics are how NL directs people and organizations towards excellence (some of these metrics are outlined in the section "Metrics," page 159). They also inform the manager of her own performance as well as the quality of her decisions.

Narrative Leadership:
- helps the leader understand the stories of the people she leads
- helps the leader understand the story of the organization in which she works
- gives direction and context for creating new stories that guide individuals and the organization towards excellence
- helps the leader create an environment that works well for all involved.

What Is a Narrative Leader?

The essence of a Narrative Leader is that he adapts his leadership style to fit the needs of the people he leads and the organization he works in. His personal goal is to exemplify elegance, efficiency, and efficacy (the 3E's). His job is to help his group and each of the individuals within the group to continually move towards the 3E's.

A Narrative Leader does this by looking at the stories that people and organizations carry and observing where the stories are in harmony and where they are in disharmony. When a group of Narrative Leaders gets together to manage an organization, it produces an organization with the 3E's.

__The 3 E's__: Elegance, Efficiency, and Efficacy.

__Elegance__: An optimal and intuitively appropriate fit to the need.

__Efficiency__: No unnecessary distractions.

__Efficacy__: Produces the desired results with few, if any, undesirable side effects.

Elegance incorporates ease, and at least a modicum of joy. **Efficiency** is where the vast majority of energy expended goes towards achieving the goal, with no wasted energy. And finally, **efficacy** is the ability to achieve the goal. That is, management decisions and organizational processes enable reaching the goal.

To contrast efficiency and efficacy: we might be extremely efficient when working towards the group's goal, but the management's decisions might not enable the goal to be achieved (low efficacy). A common example of this is where a group is moving well towards producing a product, but management is not giving them either enough time or money to achieve the desired launch date. The group is moving as efficiently as it can towards the goal, but management is not being efficacious in its allocation of time and money, thereby causing undesired problems.

Through understanding the narratives of individuals, the group, and the organization, a Narrative Leader can weave together a narrative that truly works for everyone. The Narrative Leader need not have a detailed knowledge of psychology, organizational behavior, or quality assurance. These are all built into the model. The ideas that flow through NL do not require the use of this advanced knowledge.

Getting back to what makes a Narrative Leader: A Narrative Leader adapts. He looks at the situation and chooses the leadership style, i.e. the narrative, that is most appropriate at the time. His leadership narrative is constantly adapting to the environment. Certain values remain constant and give strength and structure to a Narrative Leader's style. These are:

- ethics
- care for the people he leads
- care for the organization
- care for the wider community.

A team working for a Narrative Leader feels like being seen as a unique individual with her own narrative. Being a peer of a Narrative Leader feels both comfortable and challenging: as if the NL leader is seeing the reality of situations and adapting to it, and that this leader cares deeply about how he affects the world. Having a Narrative Leader as an employee is not always easy but frequently joyful: he understands what he is doing as a leader and why he is doing it. Being a Narrative Leader takes time, energy, attention to the process of leading, and a deep understanding of oneself (and the drives and buttons that might pull one away from being present for others).

Roots of Narrative Leadership

All knowledge is rooted in prior learning. Our current moment is like the trunk of a tree. The past is the tree's roots. The future of our knowledge is the tree's branches and leaves. Narrative Leadership's major roots are:

- narrative psychology
- complexity theory
- quality assurance
- servant leadership, and
- organizational behavior.

Although these roots may seem quite disparate, they help create a simple and elegant framework from which to view an organization's dynamics and its management's behavior. Narrative psychology and its related subject, narrative therapy, approach human behavior from the viewpoint that we, as humans, are storied creatures. That is, we understand our world through stories and that all human constructs are stories within themselves. For example, the terms "sister", "brother", "mother", "father" all have stories associated with them. Each of us has our own story in regards to these constructs. In addition, we share a societal story that allows us to communicate these constructs meaningfully. It is through such stories that we understand what these terms mean and how we relate to the people to whom they refer. Our organizations and culture are shared stories.

We use stories because the world is such a complex place. Our senses are overwhelmed; therefore we create groups of data based upon how we encountered the information and the categories that we have already established. As soon as we try to put these data into context, to make meaning out of our world, we start the story-making process. This is the basis of narrative psychology. Narrative psychology brings to Narrative Leadership a framework for understanding how people and organizations make meaning out of the ever-changing chaos of our world.

David Wojick, a research engineer at the US Naval Research Laboratory, has described our present world situation as an "issue storm".

Issue Storm: *"Swirling, turbulent flows of information that blow up when people try to deal with complex issues."* [D. Wojick, "Chaos Management And the Dynamics of Information: a New Way to Manage People In Action:(Especially During Paradigm Shifts)"].

Wojick goes on to say: "Our world is increasingly dominated by issue storms. Our lives are issue driven and chaotic. Our interaction with others is complex and unpredictable" We make sense of these issue storms by looking at the world through the lens of our own story. Narrative psychology helps by giving a context for the stories themselves. In addition, complexity theory gives Narrative Leadership a way of modeling, understanding, and projecting into the future how the issue storms and narratives may interact. Much of the complexity theory that underlies NL is not discussed in this book for two reasons: a) many people are turned off by mathematics and b) the discussion of complexity theory becomes most valuable for those people who already have a strong base in NL.

For now, it is enough to note that the complex issue storms that leaders experience can be understood and handled appropriately without having to know the underlying mathematics.

The third major root of Narrative Leadership is quality assurance. One of the underlying principles of quality assurance is that processes, projects, and tasks can be best improved when tuned feedback systems are in place.

Tuned feedback: *Data about the state of a system that is easy to gather, intuitive, and timely, and that pinpoints critical needs.*

Tuned feedback not only gives information about the quality of the system, but also tells how it can be improved. When applied to Narrative Leadership, quality assurance adds tuned feedback for quickly understanding the effect of management decisions. As we tune the feedback system within Narrative Leadership, it provides us with ever more helpful information about how well we are doing as a manager of a group, as a member of an organization, and as a leader of individuals. This gives us specific feedback on what to pay attention to and how to improve the group's efficiency and effectiveness.

In many businesses the only management feedback mechanisms are the financial bottom-line and the annual reviews. These are not well-tuned metrics. Both the bottom-line and annual review metrics are ancient history. Gathering this data takes a lot of effort, and the lessons from them can be difficult to discern and to put into daily practice. Quality assurance dictates the need for quick, definitive, and efficient metrics for management.

The fourth and fifth roots of NL are servant leadership and organizational behavior, in combination these provide a loose structure from which to understand the data supplied by quality assurance, narrative psychology, and complexity theory.

Servant leadership is a management ideology that assumes that the role of the manager is to help make the worker's life better by serving the their needs before serving the manager's ego needs.

There is a wide spectrum of thinking about how to implement this ideal. Some managers implement servant leadership in a tight authoritarian hierarchy, while some others interpret the ideal as meaning that hierarchy and dictatorial rule are to be avoided. Narrative Leadership takes servant leadership's ideal and gives it a definitive form, structure, and performance measures.

Organizational behavior is a (somewhat) structured approach to understanding how organizations act and react. This comes into Narrative Leadership through some of the metrics as well as by providing leaders with a deeper understanding of their organization through the NL process (as discussed in the section "Discovering Foundational Narratives," page 91). I include lean manufacturing (aka the Toyota Way) in this mix of servant leadership and organizational behavior.

Lean manufacturing: *The process of inspecting each part of an organization and evaluating which tasks and subtasks create value for the customer, where there might be waste, and taking steps to eliminate the waste.*

Lean manufacturing takes an organizational behavior approach and attempts to eliminate all forms of waste by assisting workers in looking at how they perform their work and empowering them to make the necessary changes. Narrative Leadership takes this approach and applies it to the worker/leader interaction. Together, servant leadership and organizational behavior (along with lean manufacturing) created the initial seed for Narrative Leadership.

Narratives & Stories

In Narrative Leadership, a narrative is a special type of story:

Story: *The telling of an incident or a series of events. The telling can be oral, written, or even just thought about.*

Narrative: *A story that contains elements of the past and present, has a projection of possible futures, and the narrator is central to the storyline.*

Storyline: *A detailed description of the plot.*

For example, the Harry Potter books are stories that are not narratives. They fail the narrative test in two areas. The first test of a narrative is that the story contains elements of the past and present. That is true of these tales. The second test is that the stories tell a possible future of Harry Potter. These tales fail on this test, they give past and present, but not the future. The third test is that the narrator be central to the storyline. In the Harry Potter tales the narrator is an uninvolved third party.

Another type of story, a narrative, is exemplified by the story of our lives. It has past, present, and future. For example, the story of my life (as I tell it to myself) has a distinct past (e.g. my first dog, going to university, and patenting a basic method for PC scanners) and present (e.g being a writer, husband, and rabbi), as well as I project a possible future (such as teaching seminars on advanced topics in Narrative Leadership). In addition, I am central to my own storyline. Therefore the story of my life is a narrative.

All of us have a narrative that we tell others when people ask us about ourselves. Even if it is just "Get out of my face!" In this case the narrative is something like: "Who I am does not want you in my immediate future." The past and present are expressed in the speaker's commanding attitude and to whom she thinks the word "my" refers. The desired possible future, here, is not to have the other person around. The speaker is definitely central to the story she just told - a whole narrative in five words. Even a semi-astute listener could infer much more from these five words by adding in the context, the speaker's body language, and the tone of voice. In general, the deeper one listens to a narrative, the more the story has to say. Most of us gloss over the myriad of stories that we hear every day.

We are besieged by narratives and have learned to tune them out. The problem with tuning out these narratives is that we lose contact with reality. As leaders, we need to retrain ourselves to listen to the narratives of the people we lead. We have decades of experience at tuning them out. It will take significant time and energy to start re-hearing them.

Organizations also have narratives. Almost every piece of marketing literature is a narrative expressing a piece of the organization. The Human Resources Handbook is also a narrative of sorts. There are also unwritten narratives. These create the look and feel of the organization, and determine how it interacts with others. These are all parts of the narrative in which the (inanimate) organization is the narrator.

Narratives & Memes

Many people are becoming aware of the idea of an "internet meme" without truly understanding what a meme is.

Meme: *An idea that spreads from person to person, much like a virus. Meme's are single ideas that may combine to form a meme complex.*

Examples of memes include:
- Flags
- Hula hoops
- Stuffed animals
- Kisses
- Clapping hands.

Meme complex: *A set of closely inter-related memes that join to create something larger than each of the memes separately.*

Examples of meme complexes include:
- Religions - Catholicism, Judaism, Islam...
- Societies - western culture, Japanese culture...
- Subcultures - goth, punk, nerds, geeks....

Memes and meme complexes are important to Narrative Leaders in that they help elucidate the underlying narratives. For example, at one large firm I worked at, all the men wore ties. This meme expressed a formality and professionalism that the company wanted to show - i.e. an organizational narrative. This was also an expression of part of the company's narrative about the ease of managing a large group that all looked and thought similarly (ease of management was a major theme in this company's narrative). This meme, neckties, pointed directly to an expression of the company's narrative and indirectly to how the organization thought about people.

Expressed & Foundational Narratives

Now we are getting to the heart of this book: expressed and foundational narratives.

> **Expressed narrative**: *The truth as we tell it to others and what we want them to believe.*

> **Foundational narrative**: *The truth the individual or organization (as narrator) believes in, and upon which she makes decisions.*

These two narratives are frequently quite different. We tailor our expressed narratives to the audience we wish to influence. Foundational narratives are frequently built subconsciously throughout the life of the person or organization. Rarely do we bother to verbalize our foundational narrative; we are too busy crafting how we want people to see us.

Think of expressed narratives as our own marketing literature and the foundational narrative as the "one and only true story." These narratives are more than just the words we say; they encompass all of our communication.

Each logical entity (person, group, or organization) has only one foundational narrative. It covers all the areas of that entity's life. This narrative carries the essence of the logical entity. It is how this logical entity understands itself/himself/herself. The foundational narrative is a person's or an organization's understanding of reality.

What Is Real?

Behind the question of what is truth is the deep philosophical question of "What is real?" I won't try to answer this deep question, but will answer a related question about the definition to be used in Narrative Leadership. There are two forms of Narrative Leadership reality:

Subjective reality*: An individual's view of the world that answers the questions the individual or organization is willing to ask. That is, a relatively self-consistent narrative that operates within a self defined universe.*

Objective reality*: A massively shared view of the world that answers the relevant questions that individuals and organizations ask. That is, a self-consistent narrative that operates within an open universe of questions.*

This definition of objective reality has a fair amount of wiggle room. One question that is relevant: "What are the bounds of 'relevant' questions?" For example, science is excellent at answering questions about reality that deal with what, when, who, and how. The "why" question is not relevant to science. Questions like "Why am I alive?" Science can approach the answer of what life is and how it works, but not the underlying "why" question. (I have read many science books that use the word "why" when actually the author means "how.")

To my knowledge, no one has yet proposed a truly objective reality in Narrative Leadership terms. We continuously come upon small inconsistencies and questions that cannot yet be answered. Objective reality is an ideal to which science, philosophy, and religion all try to approach. Each has described reality with a modicum (or sometimes much more than a modicum) of subjective reality.

In this book, when I use the terms "real" and "truth" I am referring to something that approximates objective reality.

Leader vs Manager

Most managers are not leaders. The Merriam-Webster dictionary defines a manager as one who conducts business affairs while, by contrast, a leader is one who guides people. John C. Maxwell, the author of more than 60 books on leadership, says that "The true measure of leadership is influence. Nothing more and nothing less." The essential distinction is that the one works with facts, figures, and ideas while the other works with people.

> **Manager**: *A person who conducts the business affairs or operations of a group or organization.*
>
> **Leader**: *A person who guides people towards specific goals, such as excellence at her job, good communication, and understanding how she fits into the bigger picture.*

Jack Welch, retired CEO of GE, says of skilled leadership:

> When you become a leader, success is all about growing others. It's about making the people who work for you smarter, bigger, and bolder. Nothing you do anymore as an individual matters except how you nurture and support your team and help its members increase their self-confidence. Yes, you will get your share of attention from up above—but only inasmuch as your team wins. Put another way: Your success as a leader will come not from what you do but from the reflected glory of your team. [http://www.linkedin.com/today/post/article/20130708115451-86541065-how-to-think-like-a-leader]

Too many managers have trouble making the transition to leadership. Previously, they achieved a measure of success through their own struggles and expertise. Now as leaders they have to learn how to get ahead by helping other people succeed and through creating environments that reward and promote other people's excellence.

For a moment, lets look at a business as a customer might. The customer pays for the product or service, not the management of the people who make the product or provide the service. For example, when I buy a computer, I will look at the price, speed, availability, amount of memory, etc. In addition, because I practice NL I will also look at the news about how it treats the employees. I don't care if the company has one manager or ten thousand. My decision criteria are based around how well the item meets my needs and how well the company and product match my value system. I am buying a product that helps me write my books and teach my courses and I want to support only organizations that do good in the world.

Managers may make the design and production of a product faster and easier, but when I am buying a product, this is not something apparent to me. The product label does not read "500 managers helped ease this product's path to market." The product is either on the shelf and I can buy it, or it is not. All of the company's history of hiring and firing, creating time tables and design requirement does not impact my purchasing decision. Managers are expensive and do not directly bring me the product I want to buy. From this viewpoint, managers are an added expense. If I could get the same product or service without managers in the mix, I would not care. And, if it lowers the cost (because managers are high expense people) then so much the better.

From this viewpoint, managers are an unwelcome, but probably necessary, load on the company. There goes managerial ego.

Let's go back to the definition of a manager - a conductor of business affairs. Is the customer really willing to pay for this? If they had a choice, is this something they would choose to spend money on?

On the other hand, we have leaders within the company. They lead the people who do the work for which the customers are willing to pay. They guide the work and the people. They make the workers more efficient and effective. The earlier argument on the positive value of managers is really about the positive value of leaders (some of whom are managers too).

Are customers willing to pay for managers? Probably not, if they had a choice. Are customers willing to pay for leaders? Possibly, especially if the leaders enable others to make the product/service better or cheaper than anyone else's. That is, if the leaders somehow enable the product or service to be more enticing.

Note that this orientation to customer value is built into Narrative Leadership. When executives start looking at customer-oriented value, they are starting to practice Narrative Leadership. That is, executives who think about customer-oriented value are beginning to understand a major piece of the organizational narrative.

For non-profit organizations the term, "customers" are both the people being served, and the source of the funding. For most governmental agencies it is another branch (such as the legislature) or agency of the government as well as the people and organizations that are taxed or regulated. For non-governmental, non-profit organizations the source of the funding can be quite complex, including governmental agencies, other non-profits, for-profit organizations, and individuals. All of these are customers with their own narratives that contain expectations of the organization. Some of these expectations will be explicit (e.g. the contract), many may be implicit (e.g. an individual's understanding of what the contract implies, or the industry common practices). Most often, the number of implicit expectations far outnumber the explicit expectations.

For example, when I walk into a store, I expect that everything will have a posted price, that the price won't change before I get to the cash register, that there will be someone at the cash register, that I am safe in the store, that the items are legal for them to sell, that the line at the cash register won't be too long, that the method I want to pay with (debit card, cash, etc.) will be accepted, and that there will be a bag for me or some other method for me to carry my goods to the car. These are just a small subset of the implicit expectations I have when going shopping. Nowhere in it's ad or when I entered the store did it say anything about these issues - they were implicit in our relationship.

One other major difference between a manager and a leader, especially Narrative Leaders, is how they make decisions. Managers are busy people. They make tens, if not hundreds, of decisions every day. They rely on their gut instincts for guidance. Data is used to show other people that their gut decision was correct. On the other hand Narrative Leaders use data to guide their thinking, their leadership style, and their expressed narratives. Recent studies (e.g. "When Should I Trust My Gut? Linking Domain Expertise to Intuitive Decision-Making Effectiveness" by Erik Dane, et al.) demonstrated that gut level decisions tend to be correct only when the person has been in that exact situation multiple times. What is interesting in the studies is that they found that in even relatively mundane but slightly new issues, gut level decisions were more often wrong than they were right. Leaders understand that gut level decisions are driven by a person's foundational narrative. Foundational narratives are driven by past history, not necessarily a clear view of the future.

> *Most managers use data to validate what their gut tells them to do. Leaders use data to guide their thinking in the formation of new chapters to their foundational narrative.*

LEADERS: THOSE WHO ARE AND THOSE WHO THINK THEY ARE

Recently, I had two great opportunities to witness the actions of leaders. One was an example of leadership grace and the other was a person who thinks he is a leader, but isn't. The narratives between true leaders and pseudo-leaders are starkly different (see the section "Measuring Implicit Leadership (Golden Glow)," page 167 for more information on pseudo-leadership).

One day, there were four of us, that I might call "alpha dog" type leaders, all sitting around a table. We were all used to being in the leadership position, but we were quite graceful, usually, about letting one of the others lead. This enabled a far ranging discussion that elicited many creative points and significantly moved forward the business at hand. No one dominated the conversation. I also recently witnessed a contrasting situation where a second level manager, Mike, held a meeting with some of his top managers. The managers were bright and creative. When one of his managers would bring up an especially interesting point, the discussion would gain energy and the focus would be upon the person or people who had the latest interesting addition to the topic. After a few minutes, Mike would raise his voice just slightly above the hubbub and redirect the conversation just slightly. A typical topic of his was to talk about finances or other resources needed to accomplish the idea. Mike's actions would result in the energy in the room decreasing significantly and the focus would return to Mike. Mike made comments about every issue that was brought up in a meeting that lasted well over an hour. If Mike were a peacock, he would be displaying his magnificent plumage at the least provocation, whether there was a peahen around or not. Under no circumstances would Mike have let the discussion progress as it had when we four "alpha dogs" met.

> *One of the essential points of a leadership narrative is the ability to recognize excellence in others and assisting, or letting, them take the lead when it matches their area of excellence.*

Sometimes people like Mike seem to suck all of the air out of a room or all the joy out of a job. Their personal need is to be seen as the primary actor. This need is more important to them than actually accomplishing the task. Not that Mike and others like him don't want tasks accomplished. It's just that it would be a hard choice for them if they had to choose between getting the task accomplished quickly/well, and with someone else getting the kudos and control, or their own keeping of control/getting the credit, even at the expense of achieving a lower quality result.

Working for someone like Mike can be exhausting. My experience with these people is that their actions, consciously or subconsciously, are based upon a narrative that they are "less than." That is, they feel less than others who might do the task better. Less than what it takes to do the job well. Less than what they want to be. Therefore they vastly overcompensate. In the companies I have led, these were the people who had a need to be the supervisor, and then the need to be the manager, and then an executive, and then the CEO. Wherever they were, it wasn't enough. This drive and behavior might not be as apparent when viewed from below, or as a peer, but it is really blatant when viewed from higher up the hierarchy.

When I coach new executives, I warn them about up-and-coming managers that give the executive a feeling that the up-and-comer is pushing the executive around. These are the Mike-type of people. These "Mikes" are searching for some way of feeling enough within themselves. Instead of doing the introspection that it would take to truly achieve the result, they look outside of themselves. They tell themselves that this next position will be enough, or that much greater amount of money will do it. But when they achieve "this" or "that", they are still left with the feeling of being less than. So, they raise the external goal.

Mike is the type of person who will trash a group in his struggle to get ahead. If you work for Mike, realize that he won't be your boss for long. He will either move up or move on. If Mike works for you, try to reward him for selfless behaviors and penalize him for ego boosting ones. It may help. If not, assist him in moving on. If Mike is your peer, he may try to get ahead by undermining your image and then incorporating your group into his. I have seen this action more than once. See if you can assist your mutual boss in seeing Mike's behavior for what it is: external ego gratification for an internal void, and potentially damaging to the organizational narrative.

You can recognize the Mike type of character by inspecting your feelings after leaving a meeting with such a type of pseudo-leader. If you feel smaller, demeaned, or constricted, then the likelihood is that you were in the presence of Mike. I call this the "Donut Hole Manager:"

> **Donut Hole Manager**: *A person who struggles to get ahead in order to fill an unrecognized hole in their foundational narrative. For this person there is never enough to fill the hole, until he recognizes the lack for what it is.*

Leading by Talking vs Leading by Listening

It is amazing how much can be accomplished through not talking. Most of us have learned that when we want other people to do something we tell them what to do. Then we keep checking in, and give course corrections when we deem it prudent (or sometimes just because). This method worked for us as children, and it makes logical sense, therefore we translate this method into our leadership practices. We lead by talking.

The problem is that we don't put ourselves into the place of the person or people being led. We want something, we let people know. We forget that other people have their own narratives and may have excellent reasons why they are doing things as they are. This management style expects others to act as we want them to act rather than how they want or need to act. The essence of this style is that if Marvin the Manager is not getting the results he wants, he issues orders. If he is still not getting the results he wants he issues more orders. The less he gets, the more he talks.

When managing others, I have found that listening can provide at least as good results as talking. There is a time and place for listening and for talking. Managers tend to do way too much talking and way too little listening. The values of listening include:

- Gaining an understanding of the narratives at play. These narratives brought the situation to where it is today and are driving the actions, and hence the group, towards the situations of tomorrow. Through understanding of the narratives at play, a good leader can mold the desired future.
- Assisting people in feeling valued by being heard.
- Assisting the leader in seeing the world as it really is rather than how he desires it to be.

An additional asset to listening is that it creates silences. Most people feel uncomfortable with silence and will fill it with words. An astute leader can use this time to listen for what is really going on. If a leader allows silence, an easy silence, not strained with power expectations, people may fill the space with vital information. For example:

At the end of many meetings managers will ask if there is anything else to add. They look round the table, and hearing nothing quickly adjourn the meeting. In many of my meetings I would let it hang, wait a full minute, maybe even two. I was amazed at how frequently vital information came out during this interlude. Some of my doctor friends call this a "door knob confession." As the time approaches for their patient to leave, the real reason for the visit will emerge, usually just as the person is reaching for the door knob: "By the way, doctor..."

Allowing people the time and space to speak gives them respect and authority. These attributes are vital in creating a narrative that works.

EXPLICIT & IMPLICIT LEADERSHIP

We can divide leaders into two types based upon how they became a leader:

1) **Explicit Leaders**: *Leaders who are appointed by a hierarchy.*

2) **Implicit Leaders**: *Leaders who arise from a consensus of the people she leads.*

I like to view explicit leaders as being "hierarchically ordained." These people most frequently have the title of lead, supervisor, manager, or executive. If explicit leaders have training, it is frequently about operational issues. The training may include an MBA, Bachelors in Engineering, finance degree, lean manufacturing certification, etc. I have taught in many of these areas. These courses are good as far as they go. The problem is that they don't deal directly with the source of all business innovation and the source of all products and services: people.

Explicit leaders frequently come up through the ranks. They were good at one job and were promoted to the next level. Much of the time these leaders do not have the full support of the people they lead because they tend to be managers more than leaders. That is, they tend to organize data and projects rather than help people excel (see the section "Leader vs Manager," page 20).

Implicit leaders arise from a consensus of the people they lead. If an implicit leader loses the high personal evaluation of someone they lead, then they are no longer that person's leader. It's simple: if someone consistently follows you by their own will, then you are their implicit leader in that area (each of us generally has many implicit leaders that we follow). As soon as the person stops wanting to follow you, you are no longer their implicit leader.

Sometimes, implicit leaders are also the explicit leaders. That is, sometimes a manager is the person the group wants to follow. More often, a group will have an explicit leader, the manager, and another person who is the implicit leader. This second leader, the implicit leader, is followed because that person is either wise, an expert in a necessary area, or has good people skills. In the case where the implicit leader and explicit leader are different people, this can work quite well as long as the implicit leader lends support to the appointed, explicit leader.

I recently saw a case where the manager (explicit leader) was neither liked nor considered wise by the group she led. This created great turmoil within the group and a high turnover rate. Finally, an implicit leader emerged from the group. The implicit leader fully lent her support to the manager. This stabilized the group and allowed it to work around the foibles of the manager.

Implicit leaders tend to have an ability to bring people together. It's not always that they are the most likable, the most extroverted, or the greatest expert. Implicit leaders have a sense of the narrative of the group. With new technology, this can be trained. Most often, though, it's something the implicit leader has developed in a patchwork of self-education.

Technology*: In Narrative Leadership terms, technology is a structured process for modifying foundational narratives.*

Examples of Narrative Leadership technology include:
- Pay raises and promotions
- perks including a better office, new computer, new chair, better health insurance
- Conscious use of "door knob confessions"
- Neurolinguistics and neuropsychology
- Change of leadership style (see the section "Leadership Styles," page 101).

These technologies can be used by any leader, explicit or implicit. The proper use of Narrative Leadership technologies can greatly increase a group's 3E's: elegance, efficiency, and efficacy.

To sum up this section: An explicit leader is appointed. An implicit leader arises from the desire of the people to follow.

REAL LIFE EXAMPLES

Websites are examples of expressed narratives and are a good place to look for foundational narratives. They are a demonstration of an expressed narrative. The website is crafted to create an impression. But the decisions that went into crafting this narrative are part of the foundational narrative. It's like being on a speedboat. When you look back, you'll see a big spray of water. From this spray, you can infer some things about how the boat is powered, such as it probably has a big engine and a propeller. This may not be everything you might want to know about the boat (or foundational narrative), but it is a good starting point.

Figure 1: Home Page of Website: www.NarrativeLead.com

Doing a quick analysis of my website, www.NarrativeLeadership.info, there are a few things that stand out (besides that this is a black and white rendition of a colorful webpage). The picture at the top of the webpage stands out. It's a photo I took several years ago on a trip up to Alaska. It reminds me of family and friends, beauty, good times, and the very beginnings of what has ended up as this website. My expressed narrative here is to show beauty and the hint of more – that there is more behind, or in, this photo than can be seen in a quick glance, i.e. a narrative.

I crafted the expressed narrative to give the reader a quick feel for what I and Narrative Leadership are about. My decisions were based upon the market segment I wanted to attract, i.e. people who were looking for more in their lives and their business.

This website is part of starting a new venture, and resources are limited. So part of my present foundational narrative is a sense of limited resources: limited time and limited money. My foundational narrative immediately eliminated the universe of professional photographers as being too costly. Since I greatly value my integrity, I also eliminated the possibility of going on the internet to find and use someone else's pretty picture. I quickly scanned through my photos and this one stood out.

There are clues in the picture that it is not a professional photo. The contrast is a little too stark and there is no photographer's signature or copyright. Also, the water slants off to the left, i.e. the camera was not quite level when the photo was taken. It's these small things that help point out the big thing: the foundational narrative.

Therefore my foundational narrative includes beauty, integrity, and a sense of limited resources. Beauty, integrity, and resource limitations narrowed my choice of photos from which I could craft my expressed narrative. I wasn't going to go to a professional photographer. I wasn't going to choose a picture that wasn't beautiful. I wasn't going to pay someone else to use their photo. And, I wasn't going to steal someone else's photo.

As someone new to Narrative Leadership you might come upon my page and see the photo at the top and the blog posts below it. Notice that the blog posts are first while the "About" page and "Contact" page are secondary pages. The other pages are also expressions of my expressed narrative. As a Narrative Leader, you should be asking: Why this organization? Why this picture? Why all the white space? Why isn't he charging but instead giving all this information away for free?

These follow-on questions point to my foundational narrative around Narrative Leadership. For me, NL is my legacy. It is a gift I give to the world, unsure of where and if it will take root. The best way that I know of for NL to grow, is to sow lots of seeds, throw them into the wind, and see who responds. I leave lots of breathing room for people to accept parts or all of this, at their own speed. Therefore, no sales pitch, lots of good info, lots of white space.

I can hear some of my friends saying: "But you're special. You thought this all through first and then designed the site to meet your needs." True, I did think about who my market was before designing the site. But most of the decisions listed above were subconscious, just like everyone else.

> *Most decisions that stem directly from the foundational narrative are subconscious decisions, not rational and well thought through.*

In my life I've tried to bring together my expressed narratives and my foundational narrative. Like everyone else there are parts of my life that I'd rather not have people know (like when I've done something truly embarrassing). But what I have found is that when my expressed narrative and my foundational narrative are fairly close together, people trust me more. Put another way, when I do what I say and I say what I do, it gains trust. As a consultant, writer, manager, and teacher, trust is my stock in trade. Therefore I pay special attention to my expressed narratives and work to understand more of my own foundational narrative. This is evident in my website in the amount, style, and type of personal sharing that I do. It is carefully thought through about what personal information is shared and what is not.

Without at least a modicum of trust you would not be reading this. Without my coworkers trusting me, my life would be so much harder. Without trust no one would come to my classes or buy my consulting services. Therefore:

> *To have an integration (i.e. integrity) between your expressed narrative and your foundational narrative is good marketing.*

LEADERSHIP

True leadership has its own narrative. This can be summed up as:

> **Leadership narrative**: *Creating a story that works for all of the stakeholders.*

Stakeholder: *Any entity that has an interest in the organization. This includes employees, shareholders, the community in which the organization resides, and regulating bodies.*

The first question is what do I, the organization, and the people I lead mean by "work." I've known many people who think that getting to know their coworkers better is work related. I've also know many managers who think that this type of "personal business" is not to be done on company time. However, most leaders are not on "company time" when they do some of their hardest work - they are relaxing or doing something completely different when a solution comes to them for one of the hardest problems they had been facing.

As an example, a few decades ago, I was working for a large company. In one of the groups I led, there was a subcontractor (who I'll call Sam) that was having an especially bad day. At lunch, he was going down in the elevator, listening to a couple of vice presidents talking. Sam blew his cork, told the vice presidents off, and told them he was going out to the car to get his gun (no kidding).

The VP's rode the elevator back up to my floor. I was waiting for it so I could go down. They informed me what had happened. I called security who immediately shut the building down and called the police. So far everyone, except Sam, was acting out of their foundational narratives fairly cleanly. We told the right people about the incident so that people could be safe. Good reactive leadership.

Of course people in the building heard about the incident. When a thousand or so people are locked in a building, rumors fly. Most of the rumors had nothing to do with the reality of the situation.

Now was the time for true leadership to emerge. People were frightened. Our place of business had moved from a workplace to a "let's get out of here" place. The senior managers met and they decided that the "best" thing to do was to say nothing unless someone asked us a specific question. Then we were to just that question and not volunteer any further information. I was the lone dissenting voice.

My opinion was that we needed to get ahead of the situation. The only way that we could keep this a safe and creative workplace was by letting people know what happened, what we had done about it (the police already had the man in custody), and what people's options were (work from home for a few days, be escorted to and from their car, take a few days off as long as it was okayed by their manager, or see a therapist at our expense). I thought that my way of handling the situation would make people more at ease, not less. The consensus opinion was that we, as managers, were not trained to handle the situation. If people brought it up, we could then direct them to people that were trained. I was allowed to handle the event the way I felt best within my own department.

Looking at this in Narrative Leadership terms, there are four things that stand out:

1) Expressed narrative #1 of the majority of the senior management: We, as managers of the work environment, are unequal to some parts of our job.
2) Expressed narrative #2 of the majority of the senior management: If we don't talk about it, the problem may go away.
3) Foundational narrative of all of us managers: We, as managers of the work environment, feel unequal to this task. (We all felt overwhelmed by this event.)
4) None of us, including me, asked "What was it about Sam's foundational narrative and this work environment that set off this event at this time?"

This was not the end of this affair. Sam was released on bail a few days later. He then called in two bomb threats over the next two weeks. Each time we were forced to clear the building. He was finally re-imprisoned and the threats stopped. What was amazing to me is that the other senior managers stood firm on our policy about handling the situation.

I set about talking to everyone in my department, informing them of all that had transpired and their options. Then, I listened to how they felt, and what might help them feel safer. As you might imagine, rumors were rampant. People throughout the company, many not even in this building, were talking to people in my department to find out what was happening. When the second bomb threat was called in, people called my managers to find out if it was real and what they should do about it. They called us, rather than their own senior managers or the security office. We had become the "safe harbor" of straight and full information.

As a leader in the company, I now had another issue to handle. By my unique way of handling the situation, I had unbalanced that delicate balance of power that goes on in most companies. Many people within the company saw me as somehow "more than" others of my level of seniority. If, at the time, I had NL metrics at my disposal, I would have known to pay attention to this (see the section "Metrics," page 159). This unbalance made it harder for me to negotiate with my peers. Many of them (like most people in the world) have a sensitivity around feeling "less than."

In hindsight, one of the easiest things I could have done was to have taken a week or two of vacation. Much of the glamor of being unique would have dissipated without my presence there to feed it.

When power shifts within an organization, opposing forces develop. Frequently the opposing force will be disproportionate to the initial shift.

Usually these forces are subconscious reactions from people's foundational narratives. People may try and rationalize their actions, but these are generally after-the-fact rationalizations, rather than true driving causes. The purpose of the explanation is generally to divert attention from the true cause. It is my experience that the underlying purpose of these forces is not to re-equalize the situation, but to make those who gained pay a disproportionate cost for their gains.

Diversion narrative: *An expressed narrative crafted to divert others from searching further for the foundational narrative.*

Image narrative: *An expressed narrative crafted to show the person or organization in a certain light. This is the majority of expressed narratives.*

Clear narrative: *An expressed narrative that is a clear expression of the underlying foundational narrative.*

Diversion narratives can be very tricky. In the example with Sam the subcontractor, management had a diversion narrative prepared. If anyone wanted further knowledge or assistance, we were to respond only to the direct question. In this case the diversion was twofold:

1) "We're not telling you more because there is no more to tell."
2) "We have it all handled, because look - here's the resolution to your question."

After some experience with NL, many people are easily able to distinguish the difference between a diversion narrative, image narrative, and a clear narrative. Some of the methods to distinguish between these are outlined in the chapter "Discovering Foundational Narratives," page 91.

When a leader learns to recognize the different types of expressed narratives she gains three advantages:

1) The leader has a clearer view of the situation and can act and react accordingly.
2) The leader has access to how people want to be seen. Therefore she can be more effective, efficient, and elegant in her communication with the group.
3) The leader is not misled by the craftsmanship that went into an employee's expressed narrative. Noting the

craftsmanship, she can use that craftsmanship to ease the communication.

Here are two short examples of advantage #3:

I had two employees. Ethel thought of herself as brilliant and well educated, and expressed this by constantly quoting famous authors and philosophers. Eric, on the other hand thought of himself as very down-to-earth, and oriented towards nature. Eric interwove into his conversation things about his garden, hunting and fishing trips, and other nature facts. So when I was going to be talking with Ethel, I would prepare myself with some pithy new quotes, and when I talked with Eric, I would briefly bring in something interesting about being in nature. The harder the discussion was to be, the more I would interweave details from their own crafted narratives. That is, for Ethel, I would prepare more quotes and philosophical ideas that supported what I wanted to communicate. For Eric, I would frequently use similes about gardening - a time for sowing seeds, a time for pulling weeds, etc.

The ideas behind this are:

- *People spend a great deal of energy in developing and maintaining their image narrative. They have a stake in being seen that way.*
- *When people are comfortable, they can usually listen more deeply and incorporate what is being said.*
- *Join people where they are, first. Then lead them, at their speed, towards excellence.*

As a leader, it's of great value to understand where your efforts can be put to best use, i.e. understanding the foundational narrative. As consultants it can also be of use in avoiding situations that are likely to lead to disaster.

ORGANIZATIONAL

It's been fascinating for me as a smalltime investor to read the literature companies put out to persuade me to buy their stock. Even the legal filings to the SEC are all aimed at putting the company in the best light possible. They are carefully crafted image narratives within the legal framework (and with the fear of lawsuits). What's true about these narratives is that no matter how carefully crafted they are to misdirect or divert attention, they always point towards the foundational narrative. It is just a matter of gathering together a series of expressed narratives and looking for the common thread.

Early on in the development of NL, I would peruse various companies' stock prospectuses, annual reports and marketing literature. I would then try to outline the various expressed narratives and the underlying foundational narrative. I'd watch the company for the next few months and see if its major decisions were in agreement with my understanding of their foundational narrative. It was a great learning tool. From this developed some of the methods listed in the chapter "Discovering Foundational Narratives," page 91.

I have used NL to aid my work as a consultant and as an employee. Many years ago, I consulted with Enron. Enron's expressed narrative was fairly consistent as expressed by the CEO: "[We plan to transform] from a natural gas and electricity trader, transporter and wholesaler into a competitive electricity retailer" and "We have a chance to create an AT&T for the electricity business." Grandiose statements, but what do they really mean? Many of Enron's public expression were like this. Enron put its name on a football stadium and ran Super Bowl ads. Its offices were high-tech chic and the executive suites were elegant. All of its communication seemed to say, "We are doing really well now, and soon we will be amongst the biggest and best."

As somewhat of an insider, I was able to see that the expressed narrative did not completely reflect the foundational narrative. That is, what Enron communicated was not how decisions were made. One verbalization of their foundational narrative might be "We are the next big thing, and we are going to remake the energy industry in our image." Ego. Bravado. Enron could not fail because whatever it did, the industry would follow. Enron hired very young people to be vice presidents (the foundational narrative: "Being young, they must understand this Internet thing"). Enron had many vice presidents in their mid to late 20's who had no experience in the energy industry. Enron bought small software consulting companies with revenues of $1 to $10 million and appointed their owners as vice-president's of a $60 billion energy trading company. Enron was over 6,000 times bigger than the companies these executives were used to managing. The executive team had little experience and gave no consistent directions except "up." They had no goal except to make it big. They had no definition of boundaries except "Move over everyone."

In brief, Enron's expressed narrative was:
- "We are great and we're going to be big."
- "We know what we're doing, where we're going, and how to do it. So either help or get out of the way."

Their vague but grandiose expressed narratives pointed towards a main topic in their foundational narrative:
- "We don't know where we are going, but with enough bright people we will get there."

They relied upon the interaction of these bright young executives to create a gold mine. In fact several executives said that this rough and tumble interaction was a corporate measure that they were on the right track:
- "Irritation and stress are hallmarks of a company that's on the move."

What impressed me the most in my short time there was that they were moving fast. It was more like an exploding bomb, going everywhere at once, instead of an arrow directed towards a target. I kept my time working with Enron quite short. The disfunction inherent in their foundational narrative was one of the few clear things about Enron.

SOCIETAL

Every year in the USA, around tax time, the societal narrative changes from its normal routines to one of taxes. The US Congress talks a lot about tax fairness and tax effects upon the economy. What Congress does not talk about is the effect that taxes have on narratives of the people being taxed. Both our foundational narrative and our expressed narratives are affected by taxes. We talk a lot about how we hate taxes, or how unfair they are, or how they stymie innovation (all expressed narratives). In addition we have to plan for them, and we may feel angry or frustrated by them (both foundational narratives).

I have never met anyone who likes the taxation process, no matter how much he supports what the taxes are spent upon. In all of Congress' work to make a tax system that helps the right things, we have created a system that people hate.

To put it simply, government has created a system that draws people's ire (a negative expressed narrative). No company would exist for long with such hatred aimed at one of its main interfaces with its customers. Instead of dealing with taxpayer frustration with the system, we talk about the very real and complex problem of how taxes interact with the economy. The problem is, the interaction is so tremendously complex that no one yet has the mathematics or economics to be able to truly understand the effect of taxes on the economy. Therefore Congress argues a lot and then makes a guess that is politically tenable. The result is the continued irritation of taxpayers by having to spend many days filling out tax forms and trying to understand the "explanatory" guides. These tax forms are filled with arcane terminology that many taxpayers have difficulty understanding. This arcane terminology is part of the federal government's expressed narrative. In my opinion, the government's purpose here is to create a diversion narrative that governing and taxation are complex issues and should be left to the professionals: Congress, lawyers, and accountants. The issue that attention is being diverted away from is: "Easing the life of working adults is not a priority."

More on Expressed and Foundational Narratives

Almost all of marketing literature falls into the expressed narrative category. We want our customers to think about us in a certain way (and therefore is an image narrative - a subset of expressed narratives). Mission statements are meant to be expressions of the foundational narrative but are rarely crafted with a clear understanding of what makes an organization tick (the foundational narrative). Since much of the strategic work performed by executives and marketing personnel is about crafting expressed narratives, it only makes sense that they should have a deep understanding of narratives. Unfortunately this is rarely the case. One of my goals for NL is to help organizational leaders understand how to craft appropriate expressed narratives that reflect the underlying foundational narrative.

Like most of the rest of humanity, executives have learned how to craft expressed narratives that convince most people without the executive having an understanding of the essentials of narratives or Narrative Leadership. It's far easier for executives to craft expressed narratives that convince others than it is to actually have a foundational narrative that is a positive and attractive force. One of the main expressed narratives is the corporate measure of profitability generally called "the bottom-line."

For many decades executives have tried to convince investors that the bottom-line is a measure of how good they are as managers. That is, the bottom-line is an image narrative. As in the example below, it is also frequently a diversion narrative.

What's true is that the bottom-line is ancient history. The decisions that crafted these results were made years ago. To bring out a new product generally takes 3 to 5 years. To change an organizational strategy is a multi-year process. Almost any real change to an organization takes somewhere between 18 months and seven years. As a recent example, see the following figure outlining the cell phone manufacturer Blackberry's bottom-line (net income) versus two large decisions. (Note that Blackberry was previously known as Research In Motion, or RIM.)

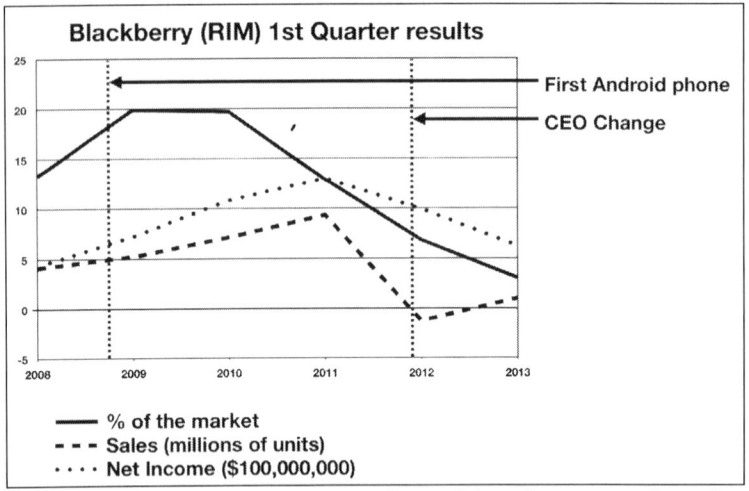

Figure 2: Blackberry's Bottom-Line with Sales & Market Share

Early this century, Blackberry had been growing rapidly. Google announced the Android cell phone operating system November 5, 2007. In late 2008, HTC introduced the first Android phone, the HTC Dream, also known as the T-Mobile G1. This was quickly followed up by seven more Android phones launched in 2009. Rather than adapt to the changed market, Blackberry decided to stay the course it was on. It took Blackberry five and a half years to come out with its response to Android, the BB10 operating system. Throughout 2009 and continuing through 2011, the executives at Blackberry kept trumpeting their successes, as more disaster signs continued: sharply falling market share, introduction of the iPad (January 2010), and finally plunging profits (huge posting losses starting in May 2010). It wasn't until these disasters were fully realized that the board acted and removed the co-presidents, Mike Lizaridis and Jim Balsillie, on January 22, 2012. This was four and a half years after their failing to react to Android and 5 years after the iPhone.

With the removal of Lizaridis and Balsillie, Blackberry was starting to awaken from its self-induced somnolence. The BB10 operating system and two completely new cell phones were in the works (Q10 & Z10), but they wouldn't be completed for another year. The new president, Thorsten Heins, received the kudos for unveiling the new cell phones and operating system on January 30, 2013.

> *The bottom-line is old news. The decisions that affected it may not have come from the current crop of managers. Managers should be evaluated on decisions they made, and their analysis of future trends, not ancient history.*

Another problem with the bottom-line is that, at least in the short run, the executive suite can manipulate it. I have seen executives push the manufacturing line to ship product this quarter, when it was actually wanted by the customer in the next quarter. This helped <u>this</u> quarter's bottom-line but hurt next quarter's bottom-line and also hurt the customer relationship (from the customer's view: being billed now for items that were in the next quarter's budget and having to store the equipment until the facilities were built for the equipment). I've seen executives move products into finished goods inventory that were by no means finished, but by the company's accounting practices it effected the bottom-line in a positive way. There are many tricks that can be played with the bottom-line. None of them make the company a better company to work for, make the products better, or show the excellence of the decision-making capabilities of the executive suite.

The bottom-line has become the most favored, and the most feared, of the measurement tools available to executives. The problem for everybody concerned is that the bottom-line really does not show the quality of the organization's management. In the 1940s and the 1950s, when we viewed companies as being little clockwork mechanisms, the bottom-line seemed a perfect measure. We put in all the raw components at one end and out the bottom end comes the bottom-line, demonstrating the quality of each of the little gears inside this mechanistic organization. This idea of the bottom-line has become so integrated into the social narrative that it has become a meme. This meme refers to the essence of an idea or issue: "Just give me the bottom-line." Our narrative around the bottom-line is : "the bottom-line is the heart of all that matters."

> *Be wary of the bottom-line. It tells you about ancient history, not about the current state of affairs.*

In a later chapter (see the section "Metrics," page 159) are outlined some of Narrative Leadership's responses to the current vacuum of measurements of good management. For now, suffice it to say that the bottom-line is not a measure of the foundational narrative. The bottom-line has become an expressed narrative and social meme, rather than a true measure of the foundational narrative.

> *We pay far too much attention to the bottom-line and not enough attention to hiring, training, and keeping good leaders.*

Foundational Narratives

Foundational narratives are the basis for all decisions a person or organization makes. The purpose in understanding the foundational narrative is so that we, as leaders, can understand the decisions that are being made and influence future decisions, moving the person or organization more towards excellence.

The foundational narrative is the entire story of the person or organization, from inception to conception to growth and continuing until death. It is a complex, organic story that changes with time and events. Some parts are like pinwheels, spinning with the least breeze. Some parts appear to be the bedrock upon which the individual's (or organization's) personality is built.

> ***Adaptive narrative***: *The part of a foundational narrative that changes with the environment, i.e. context sensitive.*

> ***Core narrative***: *The part of a foundational narrative that is slow to change or changes only with major life events.*

We can think of narratives as being on a linear scale. On one end is the image form of expressed narratives. Image narratives change quickly - slight changes in the audience, time of day, setting, emotions, and thoughts can create vastly different image narratives. On the other extreme is the core form of foundational narratives. Core narratives take huge events or great dedication to change.

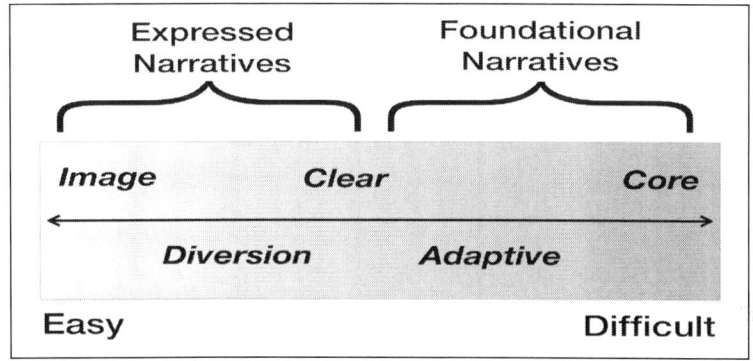

Figure 3: Ease of Changing the Different Types of Narratives

Adaptive narratives also change over time, but much less than expressed narratives, but more easily and quickly than core narratives. The adaptive narrative is how we are making decisions at the moment, unlike the expressed narrative. The expressed narrative is not about how we make decisions, but how we want to be seen. Growth and gaining wisdom are part of the adaptive narrative.

The core narrative is a combination of the part of ourselves that we value most highly combined with the part of ourselves that we really don't want to look at. These two parts combine to form one solid core that changes slowly and is rarely deeply analyzed.

The important part, for this introduction to Narrative Leadership, is that as a leader you are always dealing with both parts of the foundational narrative. The more you can understand the core foundational narrative, the more accurately you can predict long-term decision trends. The more of a feel you have for the adaptive foundational narrative, the better you can predict and handle the daily issues. For example:

I knew a manager, Marge, who had an anger issue. Most of the time, if she was asked a question, Marge would assume that she was being attacked, and reply with a return attack. Even simple questions, like "Do we have any copier paper?" might elicit an attack: "Have you used up all of the paper?" Part of Marge's core narrative was "All questions are questions about my right to be a manager." Another part of her core narrative was "When someone shows interest in my children and grandchildren, they are probably a friend." As Marge's employees learned about her core narrative, they used one aspect of it to help with the other (and thereby creating an adaptive narrative for themselves). Before asking any questions a knowledgeable employee would look around Marge's office for new pictures of her family. The employee would talk with Marge about the photos, then ask if there was any more copy paper. This may seem a round-about process, but it was much shorter and easier on all concerned than just outright asking.

> *A Narrative Leader adapts to the reality of the situation and tries to make the best of it. Therefore, the first task of a Narrative Leader is to discover what is real.*

Narratives & Internal Politics

I have frequently heard people say that they hate the politics that occur in their workplace. When I probe deeper, I usually find that what they are troubled by is that someone or some group is gaining at the expense of the good for other people, groups, or the organization. In NL terms:

> **Politics**: *The interplay of the narratives of the various participants.*

Politics is always going on whenever two or more entities interact. This is not a problem until this interplay does harm to the organization, other groups, or individuals. To denote this clearly, there are two types of politics:

Operational politics: *The normal give and take of the interplay of narratives where the outcome is positive for the organization and no group or individual is significantly impacted negatively without her consent.*

Ego-based politics: *The interplay of narratives where the outcome for one group or individual comes at the expense of the organization, other groups, or another individual without her willing consent.*

All political actions and statements are expressed narratives. In most instances, though, they are a great indicator of the underlying foundational narrative. This is especially true of ego-based politics (I'll talk more about when this is not true in a moment). In general, a person makes ego-based political moves and statements to fulfill a need in his foundational narrative. That is, he has a hole in his narrative that he is trying to fill with this political ploy. Here is an example of ego based politics in which I became involved:

A moderate size private nonprofit organization brought me in as a consultant. Charlie, the head of the organization, wanted to move Mary out of operational management. In addition, twice in the past two months there had been a physical confrontation between clients and staff. It was unclear to the staff about how to report these incidents. Therefore the appropriate forms had not been filled out. Charlie's expressed narrative was that the organization had just had two quality control issues that they were going to have to report to the contracting agency. This would not look good and might make it harder to get funding next year, especially with the tight economic times.

This expressed narrative had three layers (as do most ego-based political ploys):

1) ***Overlay***: *The part of the expressed narrative that contains what looks like objective truth.*

2) ***Spin***: *The part of the expressed narrative that moves the narrative from the overlay towards the desired goal of the foundational narrative.*

3) ***Nucleus***: *The part of the expressed narrative that contains the clear expression of the foundational narrative. Frequently the most significant part of the nucleus is the desire for power.*

In this case, the overlay was that there had been two quality problems. The spin was that it would create significant problems in the future. The nucleus was that Charlie felt challenged by Mary and wanted to put distance between them. I was brought in to make sure that there were no more quality issues of this sort, i.e. deal with the spin issues, and to help Mary adapt to the changes that would be required by the nucleus of Charlie's expressed narrative. That is, "What can we do about our quality issues, and while you're at it, help me move Mary aside and help her accept the necessity."

Upon looking into the situation, I found that Mary was well respected within the organization and was doing a reasonable job, given all of the constraints. The quality errors were systemic, not just in Mary's department. Moving Mary aside would not cure the problem, but would increase Charlie's control of the organization. And finally, Mary did not want to move aside. Therefore, this was a typical ego-based political move.

After pulling apart the three layers of the expressed narrative, the next task was to try to understand what the nucleus said about the underlying foundational narrative. Therefore, I talked with Charlie, the rest of the C-suite, and a few of the other managers. What I discovered was that Charlie was preparing to retire and wanted less work managing the organization, which was very taxing for him. He knew Mary's job inside and out. By taking control of operations, Charlie had an excuse to spend less time being the Chief Executive.

Once I understood the reality of the situation, I was then able to propose a set of solutions that would address the true and the stated issues. Addressing one of the stated issue was easy: I proposed a quality assurance process with a feedback system. Addressing the true issue was much more difficult since Charlie did not want to openly state that he wanted less hard work so that he could ease into his retirement. Therefore, he played ego-based politics to hide the true issue. His retirement plans were part of his core narrative. He was unwilling to look at them or even express them cleanly. Charlie had reached his level of incompetence and wanted to retire-in-place.

Retired-in-place (RIP): *Someone who has reached a place of comfort, and is unwilling to continue to learn and advance.*

Let's return, for a moment. to the issue of when ego-based politics do not directly relate to someone's foundational narrative. Game players and sociopaths play the political game for little other reason than that they enjoy it. Some psychologists claim that behind it all is a deep-seated rage against the world.

In general these people have the following characteristics:
- Are charming
- Have poor impulse control
- Like to live on the edge
- Don't see other people as their peers.

These game players and sociopaths tend to find situations where their ego-based politics are either tolerated or rewarded. There are distinct NL ways of dealing with game players and sociopaths, but it is beyond the scope of this book. Talk to an NL mentor or take an advanced class for help in these situations.

Leadership Narratives

What does it mean to have a leadership narrative?

The definition of a leader varies from culture to culture. In some cultures a leader is defined as someone who is strongly authoritarian, i.e. has control. In some other cultures, a leader is defined by someone who assists others. Some cultures expect leaders to have a firm vision while other cultures may expect leaders to develop vision in those they lead. When looking at the narrative behind all of these definitions, one thing stands out:

***Leadership narrative** (alternative definition): The purpose of leading is to enable others to excel within the group framework. (Compare this with the "Leadership narrative" definition on page 32)*

There are personal foundational narratives that state, "Leadership is about getting other people to help me excel." This is essentially an ego-political narrative to which many dictators adhere. From a cultural viewpoint, this is a losing narrative. It serves the individual at the expense of the culture. The narrative behind this is not one of enabling others, but of using others. Therefore this ego-political narrative is not a leadership narrative but a user narrative.

***User narrative**: The purpose of leading is for the leader to gain kudos.*

The core foundational narrative of a leader is the accomplishment of the group's goals and the enhancement of the individuals. The core foundational narrative of a user is "more." There is never enough – never enough power, never enough money, never enough to fill the user's need. A true leader can progress at the pace of the group, while a user is driven by the pace of her need.

Therefore, one of the ways of telling if someone is a user or a leader is by the pace at which she guides others. A true leader's pace ebbs and flows with the needs of the tasks at hand and of the individuals she leads. Conversely, a user's pace varies according to her own internal needs, unrelated to the task at hand and the needs of others.

I once had a boss who had a user narrative. He had been a fighter pilot and was used to fast paced decisions. He liked to apply constant pressure, increasing it only when it might suit an attack plan that would benefit him. For example, he frequently tried to gobble up other managers' teams. As he would start to hatch a plan he would put pressure on all his people to work harder so that he could take a few people off their tasks to help him plan his takeover of this other group. When the takeover was accomplished he rarely returned the people to their prior tasks and task levels, but would assign the people he had used in the attack to new tasks. This left the rest of the group at the frantic pre-takeover pace. All of this created a high stress/high turnover environment within the group.

> *The art of leadership is not the art of war. The art of leadership is searching for the greatest good for the largest number of stakeholders while ensuring that those who might "lose" are included in as part of the solution.*
>
> *There are no winners and losers in leadership. If anyone feels like they are losing, the leader has, to some extent, lost too.*

Part of the foundational narrative of the leader is that she is a leader for everyone in the group. It's natural for a leader to like some people more than others. As a leader, though, she doesn't just lead those people she likes. She leads the whole group. Some people have a natural ability to hold the narrative of the group as a set of individuals as well as an entity in its own right. Most of us tend towards one extreme or the other:

1) Seeing the group as only a set of individuals - Therefore the narrative of a leader centers around the relationships.
2) Seeing the group as only an abstract entity - Therefore the narrative of a leader centers around tasks.

Narrative Leadership is the middle ground. The group is both a set of individuals and has a narrative of its own - The narrative of a leader balances relationships with tasks. Leadership is a foundational narrative that yields a work environment that is both effective, efficient, and most of the time enjoyable..

Some people have a knack for leading. They lead and others naturally follow. These leaders may not be conscious of what they are doing that makes other people want to follow. For most of us, a leadership narrative is a conscious effort.

Even someone who has a knack for leadership can significantly improve her results if she applies her mind to the to the profession of leadership. This conscious crafting can significantly differentiate her from mangers that do not have her insights into leadership. In good times she may be a little more proactive, have a little further insight into future possibilities, and her group may be a little more effective. In bad times she will be the go-to person. She will see the way of combining opposites to make something stronger and better. One of the strongest parts of her foundational narrative as a leader will be this "And" in regards to opposites rather than "Either this, or that. But not both."

Sharks

As an ex-oceanographer, I know this does a disservice to sharks. But bear with me. This does work as a social meme.

> **Shark**: *A person who attacks as part of their foundational narrative. The attack is not cause related or context related, but related to the stories that are going on internal to the individual.*

I have run into sharks more than once. Some people believe that sharks are everywhere while other people want to believe that sharks are just figments of other people's imaginations. My experience is that sharks are real, extremely dangerous, and relatively rare. The reason for bringing up sharks at this point in the narrative is that the actuality that sharks are out there needs to be part of the leaders foundational narrative.

A shark will try to attack what he considers to be your most vulnerable place. We see this in politics quite frequently where attack ads strike with partial truth while the perpetrator(s) hide behind a grand sounding organizational name. This also happens in business and nonprofits. It's rare, but it's startling when it happens. The more the leader stands out, the more likely a shark is to come along.

The best defense against a shark is honesty, integrity, and knowing thyself.

The second best defense against the shark is distance.

Distance can work fairly well. Distance in level. Distance in physical space. But sharks can come from miles away. When a shark feels the need to feed, it will search high and low for a target.

The pain that a shark bite incurs can be so overpowering that sometimes nothing else seems to exist except the shark and the pain. At other times a shark bite can be no more than an unexpected flea bite. The difference is not in the attack, nor in the attacker. The difference is in how well you know yourself. As a leader, the better you know yourself the less ease people have in knocking you off the pedestal that they have placed you on.

If you are a peer of a shark your best defense is to have everyone know who you are and that you consistently act ethically and with integrity. In this case the best defense is the truth. There are two natural reactions that people have when they sense a shark is near: 1) to try to make friends with the shark so that it won't attack, or 2) try to pretend that this shark doesn't exist. Neither of these approaches is effective against a shark. In the first case the shark will get to know your weaknesses better and be able to strike more effectively. In the second case he may take you for a snob and single you out. My experience says that the best course is to maintain as much distance as possible, while paying close attention to what the shark does and says.

I haven't seen too many bosses attack people in their own group. Maybe because it's too easy. If your boss is a shark, my suggestion is the same as if he was a peer: keep your distance, and keep your eye on him.

I've had sharks working for me. They are dangerous employees. As his group leader, you're an especially easy target. He has many opportunities to gather information about your weaknesses. I'm not sure how to reform sharks. It appears to be part of his core narrative. That is, his shark behavior can be changed only slowly or with a sudden shock to his system. Your best bet may be into assisting him in finding a position that fits him and is somewhere else. Barring that, always have meetings with him with a third party present. Always. Remember these are sharks you're dealing with.

Because sharks rarely show their nature in an interview, the options are either good telephone interviews with their references or human resource policies that assist sharks in leaving the organization. Since most people, including human resource managers, would rather not think about sharks there are a few organizations that have good policies to help managers relieve themselves of sharks. What happens most often is that the shark get shuffled between departments. With each shuffle, the shark gets angrier and gathers more information about who and how to strike next.

The downside of leadership is being exposed. There is no preventing people from gossiping, making up tales, or just being sharks. But the defense for these is also a tremendous aid towards being a better leader. Once again it is: know yourself.

It used to be that seeing a therapist or psychiatrist was thought to be the end of one's career, a huge weakness. For years I have counseled that anyone starting a business is crazy unless they have a therapist – the stresses are just too hard. What I am talking about here is not about illness at all. It's about making yourself better. It's the difference between a weekend athlete and a pro athlete. The weekend athlete feels that he knows the game pretty well. A pro athlete never feels that she knows the game well enough. A pro is always looking for the edge to be better. As a leader, your tool is you and your narratives. A pro athlete would find the best trainer, coach, and physical therapist that she could find. A professional leader makes her life and her leading ability so much greater when she surrounds herself with the best professional coaches, consultants, and therapists that she can find. It is a matter of enhancing your own career – making things better for you.

First, lead yourself.

Few leaders take the time and effort to understand themselves well enough to know how they effect others. Take the case of the average manager, she has an idea of where she wants her team to go and she lets her team know through verbal and written communications. The words are meant to convey the message of where the team is to aim. The problem is that the stronger communication mode is nonverbal. For an untrained leader the nonverbal messages that she is sending out are probably in conflict with the verbal part of the message. Her communication is inefficient. For example, she may be saying and implying "Do this because it will enhance your career." Her nonverbal message may be "Do this because it will enhance MY career." A quite different message that probably won't increase the worker's efficiency.

If our foundational narrative and our expressed narrative are not in alignment people not only get mixed messages, the louder message is the foundational narrative. That is, how the manager decides what is rewarded, and what is punished is, usually, vastly more important than what is said. Sometimes, the rewards and punishments are extremely subtle, and sometimes they are bold, as in the following example:

I knew a manager who took frequent extended vacations. Before he left he would leave a ton of directives as to what he wanted to have completed while he was gone. When he got back he would find fault with almost everything that got accomplished. The expressed narrative was "Do all of these tasks before I get back or else I will be angry." His foundational narrative was "This group cannot operate without me. So whatever new things you do while I'm away will be done wrong." After a while, his group stopped performing new tasks and just tried to maintain the status quo while he was gone. This proved effective for the group in that they were not ostracized for what they had done. This did prove frustrating for the manager, and problematic for the company.

To be both effective and efficient, a leader must understand her own foundational narrative within the workplace. This is not something we teach in our MBA programs. In fact, in my research I have found no MBA program that has a course in self-awareness. This is a fascinating lack. People are the only resource that most managers have to get work done. MBA programs are designed to fit in the ancient mechanistic view of organizations: people are replaceable cogs within the gears that are an organization. This viewpoint totally ignores the complexity of today's organizations, the complexity of our society, and the complexity of each one of us.

To be both effective and efficient, a leader must understand her own foundational narrative and how it comes out through her expressed narratives. We may never have complete knowledge of ourselves, or anyone else. But the more knowledge we have, the easier it is to lead.

CHALLENGES OF LEADERSHIP

It's been my experience that leading people with mental illnesses is one of the hardest challenges. I have never found a management or leadership book that deals with this subject head-on. According to the United States National Institute of Mental Health, over 26% of people in the USA have a mental illness. That means that if you have a group of four people together, it's likely that one of them is affected. If you lead a group of 10 people, there is a 95% chance that at least one of them has a mental illness!

In the United States, mental illness is the number one cause of disability. Worldwide the various forms of mental illness are five of the top ten causes of disability. Mental illness affects the organization through:

- Higher disability insurance costs
- Lost work days
- Loss of worker efficiency caused by the mental illness

- Loss of group efficacy caused by the leader not knowing how to effectively lead a group with members who have mental illness.

Mental illness doesn't respect titles. The Chief Executive Officer of your organization is almost as likely to have a mental illness as the lowest paid person. According to a 2007 Gallup poll, the higher the income and the more education, the better mental health people think they have ["State of the American Workplace: Employee Engagement Insights For US Business Leaders", Gallup Inc.]. But, most studies show little correlation between income and mental health. One of the things that this implies is that the higher the income the more likely it is that someone with mental illness is in denial.

The average age of the onset of mental illness is generally in the early 30s. At this age, many people have started their careers as leaders. Therefore, it is quite likely that a quarter of your peers, and possibly yourself, are affected by mental illness.

Mental illness in Western society, and especially here in the States, is a taboo subject. In fact, that is why this section is not labeled "Mental Illness in the Workplace." Too many people might have skipped over this section. Since this topic will affect almost every leader, it is important to bring this subject into the light of open discussion.

One of the things that distinguish a Narrative Leader is that he seeks out that which is real. This section is meant to be a tiny introduction into leading others who might have mental illness. I am not an expert in psychology, although I have some training that way. Also, mental illness in the workplace is not my area of greatest expertise. That said, dealing with mental illness is a part of Narrative Leadership.

Most leaders are untrained in psychology and therapy. It's a hard enough job being excellent at the work your organization does and being a leader. The workplace as it exists today is not the proper place for therapy. But as a leader you still have to deal with people having mental problems. Maybe it's someone you lead. Maybe it's your boss. Maybe it is someone from another department that you have to work with.

Recognition of the problem is the first step in making your life easier.

As I've discussed before, every leader should have a therapist, or mentor, or coach with whom he can check out his perceptions of himself. Research states that if you are a college graduate, earning over $70,000 per year, and male, then you are significantly more likely than the average person to be in denial of your own state of mental health.

I know this one excellent leader whom I'll call Marvin. Marvin had a long and distinguished career. He worked his way up the ladder to lead an organization of many thousands. Marvin had a terrible childhood. He thought that if he could build the walls around his childhood high enough and strong enough that it wouldn't affect his work or his relationships. But like any problem ignored, it festered and infected his foundational narrative. As new and exciting possibilities cropped up he'd sabotage himself or the relationship. He started drinking heavily and being highly critical of others.

Marvin had so much to offer the world, but he wouldn't let himself see it. If someone got too close, he'd have one drink too many and say something he shouldn't. Marvin still thought of himself as a leader, but he couldn't lead himself back into excellence.

Ignored problems are the arthritis of a leader. They stiffen his joints and make movement painful.

So talk to people. Assemble an accurate view of yourself. For me this is hard to do. Other people seem to see me as being much better, smarter, and braver than I think I am. I now know that I have this filter on the world. I've chosen to work on this filter so that I can see the world more clearly. As someone very wise once said "Treat others as if they have a broken heart, because they probably do." We all have hurts that alter our view of ourselves and the world around us. Recognizing these hurts so that we can see ourself more clearly is an important part of being a Narrative Leader.

The second step is research. There are a fair amount of resources on the Internet to help understand the issues of mental illness. But leading people to these resources can be problematic. With some people it may be best to be extremely gentle, others may need strong reasons to seek help. Some may respond well to suggestions to get help. Others may respond not so well and need an indirect approach. And still others may refuse even the suggestion.

I once led a very ragtag group. They were highly intelligent and high-performing workers. Every single one of them had a diagnosable mental illness. We worked well together because I had some understanding of how they would react when their hot buttons were pushed. Most of them understood that I saw them for what they were and that I valued them warts and all.

As a leader you don't have to be an amateur psychiatrist. Unless you're really well trained the attempt can be disastrous. The idea is to recognize when someone does have this handicap and figuring out a way to lead him effectively and efficiently, and help him integrate well with the group.

The third step is to get an outside view. The more minds that work on a problem, the more likely it is that you will find a high-quality solution. Talk with people you trust. Talk with people who are consciously aware of the art of leading. If you haven't had experience with leading people with mental illness, it is unlikely that you'll be able to think yourself out of the situation and into a graceful solution.

Step four is to change your foundational narrative around leading this person. It's not about changing him. Once you change how you handle him, his interactions with you and with the group will probably change also. It may not be enough, but it gives a fresh starting point. As leader, you may have to iterate through this process multiple times before finding a solution that encompasses the 3 E's (elegance, efficiency, and efficacy). To summarize the leadership challenges process:
1) Evaluate.
2) Research.

3) Apply many minds to seek what is real and what are potential solutions.
4) Change the leadership narrative.
5) Repeat these steps until you have achieved the 3E's.

Menschlichkeit

There is a Yiddish word for a special type of leader, one who leads through compassion, understanding and by example. The word is *menschlichkeit*.

***Menschlichkeit**: The art of being a graceful human being.*

A group's behavior is driven by the interaction of the group's foundational narrative with the foundational narratives of its members. With even one person within the group having *menschlichkeit*, the entire group's tone and behavior is changed. A single person's *menschlichkeit* can overcome immense hurdles. In the optimal situation the person with *menschlichkeit* will be the group's leader or manager. People will naturally be drawn to this person and will have an easier time following the *mensch (*someone who embodies *menschlichkeit)*. If someone else within the group has *menschlichkeit* and the manager does not, the group's members may be split between following the natural leader or following the organizationally imposed manager.

Being a *mensch* and a leader is not being breezy and full of lightness. The task of a leader is extremely broad while requiring great focus, is full of day-to-day tasks, requires significant drive towards long-term goals, is filled with personalities and politics, and requires a deep knowledge of oneself. *Menschlichkeit* is a developed trait. To learn it takes desire, practice, knowledge of oneself, and deep listening to the foundational narratives that abound around us. Leaders need not have religious faith in order to be a *mensch*. What is necessary for a leader is to be able to:

- Get outside of herself
- Orient her thinking towards creating an environment that works well for all involved

- Know the art of deep listening
- Balance goals, environment, people, and joy.

Of all the managers that I have worked for, were my peers, or worked for me, only one has embodied *menschlichkeit*. Extremely few managers allow themselves to get outside of their own preconceived notions long enough to deeply listen to another human being. Much of the failure lies in how we pick our leaders, how we reward them, and how we measure their success. As researchers at the University of Innsbruck state: "Self-realization is a prerequisite of a competence-oriented management" [Hinterhuber, "The Company as a Cognitive System" page 232].

When selecting leaders, organizations need a new way of choosing managers. High on the list of requirements should be *menschlichkeit*.

Cross-Cultural Leadership

Recently, I taught a course about managing organizations that cross cultural boundaries. My experience told me that the hardest part for the students would not be the cognitive lessons, but would be getting out of their own way. We are so used to our own culture that it is extremely hard not to keep falling back on our old patterns. We view the world from the narrative of the culture in which we were raised.

The class had read the text and the many short write-ups that I emailed them. Cognitively they were prepared for the exercise I was about to present. I divided the class into two groups: one was to play a manufacturing company in Bangalore, India, and the other a design company in Portland, Oregon USA. In the tee-up for this exercise they were told:

- The manufacturing line was not flowing smoothly.
- Over the past few months both companies had researched the problem.
- Each company's report laid the blame on the other company.

- Both companies were losing millions of dollars per month because of the problem.

The two groups of students were put into different rooms, and told to try and resolve the situation. I had to continually coach the Bangalore team to stay in character, it was easy for them to return to their American upbringing. But they did a good job. They had read the material, and internalized it pretty well. The American team was likewise prepared. The scenario played out for two hours, and then we met for a debrief.

The scenario had come out of a real-life situation that I was involved in a few years ago. During the debrief the same problems developed as in the real-life situation. Two of the student's comments best signify the issue. From the Portland team came the comment that they didn't understand why the Bangalore team didn't want to focus on how much they had done well together. The Bangalore team voiced extreme frustration that the Portland team just couldn't understand how relationships work and how integral they were to this operation.

From the Bangalore point of view nothing was working well. There was no relationship. All the Portlanders wanted to do was fix the problem. That's not relationship building. From the Portland point of view, they saw all the money flying out the door for every hour that they sat in meetings. So, why not fix the problem now and then worry about relationships later? This was the exact position I encountered years ago when I was brought in to resolve the issue.

This reminds me of my neighbor whose company just won a huge contract with the Indian Navy. He was warned by one of the other contractors that an upcoming initial meeting would last about 12 hours. He came to me and said that he couldn't understand how any meeting could last 12 hours. "What could be accomplished in such a long meeting?" I explained to my neighbor that he was right, few technical issues could be resolved in such a long meeting. Technically this long of a meeting is usually counterproductive. But this meeting wasn't really about technical issues, even though that is what the agenda stated. This meeting was about relationship building - to see how well they work together, how well they joke together, how they talk, how they were quiet, how they work when they are alert, and how they work when they are exhausted. This meeting was about getting to know each other.

Managing cross-cultural relationships is rarely about cognitive issues. Studying other cultures is really helpful, but unless you have a deep feeling for the other culture, your own acculturation will probably swamp your desire to think differently. This is why travel is so important. When we are in an alien environment we can begin to understand the cultural cues in which our partners are bathed. It also helps us to reflect back upon our own culture.

What we expect to see highly determines what we find.

That is, acculturation limits our ability to perceive the cues that are so clear to those of another culture. Acculturation heightens our sensitivity to certain cues and lessens our sensitivity to others. "Culture" is not only the large differences between Western and Eastern societies it's also inherent in the smaller differences between the countries, class, ethnic origin etc.

As a small-scale cultural example, I was raised near the ocean. I could sense the ocean's mood by the smell of the salt in the air and the feel of the breeze. Even if I was out of sight of the ocean I had a sense if it was a good day for surfing or offshore sailing. I was so attuned to these gentle cues that when I lived in Denver Colorado (around 1000 miles from the ocean) I was driven somewhat batty. I was so used to the salt air and ocean breeze that it's lack even penetrated my dreams. On the other hand, my wife who grew up in Philadelphia has a hard time sensing the ocean until we're almost at the beach. Whereas, for me, I can sense the ocean from here in Portland 45 miles away.

One of the main purposes of culture is to create a shared core narrative that assists us in communicating clearly and efficiently while focusing the attention upon socially important cues. In addition, this helps filter out non-essential data.

What we pay attention to determines what we miss.

Management Narratives

There are body positions and tensions that can aid or hamper the quality of our lives. For example if my shoulders are tight, it will hamper my running, depth of meditation, and ease of falling asleep. Similarly, there are positions and tensions that aid or hamper the ability to lead, manage others, and be our best self.

Few people relax into leadership positions. Most tighten up and therefore act other than from their best self. For example, I once knew a consultant who was good at what he did, well respected, and a friend to many. Being in the right place at the right time, he became president of a small company. The position, one which he had desired for many years, was too much for him. Rather than relaxing into it and finding out what people needed to do their jobs well, he sought to control their actions for "greater clarity, throughput, and keeping to the timelines." He failed the workers and they allowed him to fail (though sometimes they actively assisted in this).

After he was asked to leave, the company went on to great things. Unfortunately the stresses and recognition of his failure were too much for his emotional and psychological health.

This is not a singular story. Most managers and leaders that I have known have failed the people they led. Few recognized their failure. Most blamed it on the workers, their managers, and the tasks. In a way, my consultant acquaintance was more insightful than most. At least he recognized his failure.

Just as it would be inappropriate to ask an untrained person to climb a mountain, sit in a full lotus position, or paint a portrait, it is equally ill-advised to promote someone beyond their training, ability, and core narrative. But unfortunately this is how most managers start their career.

Lets look at person's assigned "position" in more detail. In baseball, a top-notch short stop may make a terrible catcher. Similarly, a great engineer, assembly worker, or salesperson may make a terrible manager. These positions take different talents and different training to be good at. In addition, each level of management takes different talents, mental orientation, and foundational narrative.

I have heard the argument that most anyone can be trained to be a manager if they have the desire. That's like saying that anyone can be a catcher on a baseball team. Most everyone can learn the basics, but very few have the ability to be professional at it. Organizations are staffing the management ranks as if they were pulling together a mud-lot baseball team rather than attempting to play in the major leagues. Supposedly business is all about being professional!

The problem is threefold:
- Selection of managers
- Training of managers (or lack thereof)
- The job description of managers.

SELECTION OF MANAGERS

We select managers through the use of the Peter Principle.

In 1969, Laurence Peters and Raymond Hull developed the Peter Principle. It states that a person will rise in an organization until he hits his level of incompetence. That is, managers choose a person who is the best at one job and promote him to the next higher job. At first he will not be as competent at the new job as he was at the old one. It's new, and there is a learning curve. After a while he will start to excel again. He gets promoted again and again, until he finally hits his base level of incompetence.

Most people who are suddenly promoted into a leadership position immediately reach a level of incompetence. They are new to an entirely different type of job. They were asked to make things or provide a service and now they're asked to create an environment so that other people can be excellent at the job of creating a product or providing a service. This shift is more major than most people realize.

Most of us (especially those who are from a Western culture) have a foundational narrative that the work we do is part of us. This is usually part of the core narrative, resistant to change. For example, I had an employee, Eric, who was a great programmer. When he was appointed to manage a group he found it crazy making. Nobody else was as good a programmer as he was, so his promotion left the group without their best person. As much as he tried to help other people be better, they were not as good at producing code as he had been. So he started assigning the hardest parts of the task to himself. He was then doing the job of a manager and the job of a top programmer - not able to give either task his full attention.

I see this time and time again. It's almost ubiquitous.

One of the hardest parts of management is leaving behind that at which you excelled.

Middle managers and executives don't make this change any more gracefully than anyone else, sometimes much less gracefully. In addition, they tend to make the promotion harder for others. The manager who hired or promoted a new manager tends to ignore that there's any problem "I made the shift so you can too." – No. Many of us didn't. In addition, the new manager is expected to immediately know how to do the new work as if he had been doing it all of his life.

Don't necessarily select the best technical person to become a manager. Select the person who is already leading, who has shown the ability to do the job of the next hierarchical level. Reward the best technical person in another way. Management isn't a reward, it's a profession. Then, once you've selected a person with proven leadership ability train him for the job. Assign him a mentor. Send him to conferences and classes on leadership. Give him books to read. Help him succeed.

Management isn't a reward, it's a profession.

An alternative to hiring from within is to raid another organization for its best people. There are three problems with this solution:

1) We are expecting that the other organization was better at training their managers than we are.
2) We are taking people out of one organizational narrative, where they might have worked well, and putting them into our organizational narrative where there is no guarantee that they will work anywhere near as well.
3) Rarely do we know our own organizational narrative well enough to train a new manager in it, so the new hire is automatically incompetent in working with our organizational narrative.

Corporate raiding has its own set of significant issues. It is actually much harder to learn a new organizational narrative than one might think. In addition when we cut off advancement opportunities, it creates a narrative where if people want to get ahead they know they must leave the organization.

The answer to this dilemma is in clearly looking at the organizational narrative and looking at promotion and hiring as tools that both craft the narrative of the future and express the narrative of the past. That is, look at where the organization has been and where it's going. How do the enticements used (promotion, pay increase, etc) help fulfill the organizational narrative and where have they gotten in the way? How has the organization looked at promoting from within versus external hiring, and how has this changed/warped the organizational foundational narrative? What other methods might be used to enhance the organizational foundational narrative?

In the past, organizations have used promotion as both an enticement for people doing well at their jobs and as a means to fulfill an organizational need. These are two separate expressed narratives. Frequently these are conflicting narratives. As leaders, we need to figure out ways of separating these two narratives. Not everyone wants the work that needs to be done at the next promotion level. But most everybody, wants to be rewarded for good work and dedication. In addition, the higher you go in the hierarchy the fewer jobs that are available for these rewards. It's not that fewer people are doing good work, it's that there are fewer positions available. In addition, and especially, many workers are not suited to the work necessary at the next level.

One of the biggest mistakes for line workers is that think they want to be managers. Management is an entirely different animal. Line work is any work where we actually see the results of our labor. A leader's job is to create an environment that helps other people excel as either line workers or as leaders helping still other people excel (a second level manager is a leader that creates an environment that allows other leaders to create an environment that helps line workers excel).

Over time, organizations and society need to find ways to reward good work and good workers in a way that is separate from promotion. Society currently thinks of a promotion as moving to a better job. Why can't we make the job they have better? What's true is that promotion equals a different job. It may be better in that it fits the person's foundational narrative more closely or it may be a worse job in that it doesn't fit the person's foundational narrative very well. This is especially problematic when making significant qualitative leaps as from a line worker to a manager or a manager to an executive.

Another option is a trial period. Let the person try the job and see if she likes it and how well she does at it. Make it a strong evaluation period. So many times I've seen managers let an evaluation period slide by. Many managers look at the evaluation as being just too much work or too confrontational and therefore don't do it. For this option to work the evaluation timeline must be clear to the employee and the manager. Significant and measurable evaluation criteria need to be outlined and understood by all concerned. If she doesn't meet the evaluation criteria, she can be given another evaluation period (with, perhaps, more mentoring), reassigned, or let go. In addition, it would be very helpful to have significant perks available to the individual if she decides to step back to a lower level job. If she decides to step back this should be considered a significant win for all involved. The organization has shown compassion with limits, for all to see.

A third option that some companies have tried is a technical track that parallels the management track. I've seen it work quite well. This may require rethinking the organizational hierarchy. It is probably necessary to review the organizational narrative and compare that with the promotion and hiring tools. Look at where the organization has been and where it's going. How do the enticements used (promotion, pay increase, etc.) help fulfill the organizational narrative and where have they gotten in the way? How has the organization looked at promoting from within versus external hiring, and how has this changed/warped the organizational foundational narrative? What other methods might be used to enhance the organizational foundational narrative?

For now, Narrative Leaders have to deal with the societal push for people to constantly be seeking promotion. One method is helping a worker understand her foundational narrative and where it fits and doesn't fit the current job and potential future jobs openings.

Executive Narratives

While a manager's foundational narrative revolves around creating an environment that works internal to the group she leads, the executive narrative extends this to all the stakeholders. For the executive, her orientation is not just towards leading her group, or even helping lead the company. Her orientation extends into the community, into governance, and into the future.

Not everyone is suited to this broad of an overview, while at the same time having a myriad of daily urgent tasks. In addition, there's no person above her in the hierarchy to hand out kudos. A good executive:

- Has found ways of getting her own sense of reward internally.
- Feels the organizational narrative and its effects upon the stakeholders.

- Sees where the narrative works well and where it is off kilter.
- Has the ability to put into language these differences.
- Knows how to create a change in the foundational narrative of the organization.

Most entrepreneurs and newly appointed executives have no idea how to interact with the board or the outside community. Most new execs have the common misconception that executives in general and the CEO specifically have tremendous power. She is besieged by calls on her time and attention. Every salesman, every consultant wants her attention. The people she leads think that she is all-powerful and can easily make decisions to improve their lot.

What's true is that most of the time being an executive is a nuanced position. The every action that an executive takes has an upside and a downside. The stronger, larger, more pervasive the action or decision, the stronger, larger, more pervasive the downside tends to be. A good executive strives for incorporating the 3E's (elegance, efficiency, and efficacy) into every decision. This will tend to limit the downside of decisions and actions.

The organization is like a mobile. Every decision, every change, can create major shifts throughout the rest of the organization and into the community. Big decisions, strong actions, and large changes are like strong gusts of wind that send the mobiles twisting and turning. Decisions that incorporate the 3E's are the care-filled rebalancing of the mobile.

For example, there was a CEO, Charlie, who wanted to reward a lead technician for having worked over the Christmas shut down. The technician worked the entire shut-down period in order to ensure that a shipment was not late when the plant restarted in January. Charlie was impressed with the technician and wanted to show his gratitude. Charlie thought that he could quietly give this person a bonus so that the technician would feel rewarded and acknowledged (and that the organization would run a little better because of it).

Nothing remains private for very long in an organization. Other people who had worked various parts of the shutdown period felt ignored. The lead technician's manager felt that he should have been the one to hand out the reward. And finally, the group that the technician led felt slighted. They were a conscientious group and would have also come in, if anybody had mentioned it. Therefore, they were angry with the lead technician for not mentioning it and getting this nice bonus for himself.

Charlie had just wanted to do something good. But it went against the organizational foundational narrative. It was in Charlie's foundational narrative, but not within the organization's. Because Charlie had shown favoritism, a planned promotion for the lead technician had to be delayed; otherwise there would have been too much dissension within the company. The best of intentions don't necessarily make the best of decisions.

There are no "right" decisions in business. But there are a whole lot of wrong ones.

Rather than working against the organization's foundational narrative, Charlie could have worked with the executives to institute a bonus plan for people who far exceeded what was expected. This plan would specify the person who was to hand out the kudos and under what circumstances it could be given. He could also have made this retroactive for the previous quarter. Then any manager or employee could apply for the bonus if they felt that they or someone within their group met the level of excellence required for the bonus. Alternatively, a letter of commendation could have been put in the lead technician's file, and given to him by his manager. This would not have violated most organization's foundational narrative, and would probably not have irked the technician's coworkers.

Narrative Leadership Examples

I was recently consulted about a problem between a manager (whom I'll call Mark) and an employee (Evelyn). Evelyn wanted to take off half a day on short notice. One of Evelyn's friends was getting married. The friend had been living with his fiancée for two years and been diagnosed with terminal cancer with only a few weeks left to live. They made a quick decision to marry and asked Evelyn to be part of the wedding party.

Mark quite reluctantly agreed to the time off. The business was in the process of moving offices and there was much work to be done.

The narrative of Evelyn was oriented around two life-changing events: marriage and death. The narrative of Mark revolved around task overload and not wanting to show preferential treatment.

Stepping back and looking at this from a Narrative Leadership viewpoint there are several key issues to consider:

* What would be the effect upon Evelyn if the request is denied?
* What would be the effect upon the group if the request is denied?
* Would it damage or improve the group's morale if the request is approved?

However the decision comes out, it's crucial that Mark handle the discussion with grace. The phrasing of the acceptance or denial of the request can have just as significant an impact upon Evelyn as the decision itself. In cases like this, where irreversible personal decisions are being made, it's especially important to take a moment to weigh the costs and advantages. Too many times I've seen managers make gut level decisions and create an environment in which nobody wants to work.

People don't like being treated as an easily replaceable commodity.

We like being treated as important individuals. Mark's narrative, in this case, revolved around treating Evelyn as a special case. He felt that no one should be treated as a special case. Mark's foundational narrative prevented him from seeing the bigger picture.

There was no hint of Evelyn lying about the situation. Evelyn's request had touched upon a "hot button" of Mark's.

We all become reactive at times ("getting our buttons pushed"). In this case Mark reacted to the issue of "special cases." When leading from a narrative viewpoint it's crucial to know when we are in a reactive or proactive state. If we know when we are reacting to an issue, we can take a few extra minutes, hours or days to consider how our decision is effected by our "hot button." If we know when our decisions are off-kilter, we can take the time to re-inspect the decision in light of the 3E's.

Being a Narrative Leader is not easy. At least, that's been my experience. As human beings, we are programed to create habit patterns. Habits free up our conscious, story making, mind allowing us to attend to other parts of our lives while habits take care of the more routine issues. Habits form incredibly fast. I've seen new leaders create leadership habits after only a few weeks in the position of leadership. These habits can be incredibly hard to break. But, being a Narrative Leader is about treating each person as unique and each leadership crisis as needing our total attention. Creating a habit pattern of leadership treats people like interchangeable "human resources." These habits make it very difficult to see how an individual's foundational narrative has evolved since the last time that you had interaction with him. Organizations, people, and situations evolve. Sometimes the evolution is for the better, sometimes not. For a Narrative Leader, it is vitally important to notice how the foundational narrative has changed.

In addition, habits make it difficult to switch leadership styles. Here are two examples of where I had difficulties.

I have worked with many companies that were in distress. Some were startups trying to grow quickly and some were mature companies whose foundational narrative had hit a bump. On this occasion I was working with a startup whose technology I knew well, and enjoyed. My natural tendency is to jump right in and help them resolve the technical issues and their stated management issues (the

Expert). But, this would have left the company with two leadership problems:

1) I wasn't building up their own ability to solve problems. Therefore once I left, their engineers would not have learned how to increase their own innovation skills.
2) The leaders would not have learned how to change from their own habituated leadership style. My acting as an Expert might have resolved this single issue, but would not have resolved the underlying issues of how they arrived at this crisis point.

A related Narrative Leadership issue is about my own self-leadership. One day my wife called me on her way home from a particularly horrendous business meeting. It was easy to tell how upset she was, so I suggested she hang up and put all her attention upon driving safely. Her calling before she got home gave me time to manage my own reactions to what she'd said about the meeting and shift into a mode that addressed her needs.

My basic mode of operation is to jump in and fix problems. This was not what she needed. She didn't need me to get angry at the people who acted so self centeredly at the meeting. She needed me to step back and listen as a friend and peer. I shifted from Expert leader to Peer leader. It was appropriate to the moment (and for my relationship).

Most of us adults do this type of switch in behavior quite frequently and without conscious attention. For me, it's most easy to do with my children. But it's the same process whether it's with our children, our spouse, or our coworkers. Personally, I find it most difficult when I have been emotionally triggered, such as when someone tries to hurt my wife. But I get triggered at work, probably even more often than at home. I have a long-term loving relationship with my family. I frequently don't have this with my coworkers. Since I put great value on my work, when I get triggered my reaction can be quite strong. The art of a Narrative Leader is to be able to control our own reactions, analyze the situation for what might be an optimal solution, and then act upon it.

IV. Ethics & Leadership

Every few months I read about a top manager destroying their own reputation and the reputation of the organization in which they work. I read an article about one of the top managers at Cisco who spent over $30,000 at a strip club entertaining potential customers. Larry Ellis, the CEO of Cisco, stopped payment on the credit card. Was it unethical of the manager to take customers to a strip club. Was it unethical of Larry Ellis to stop payment? Is it proper for the strip club to have to write off a $30,000 loss in income? What is each person's share of responsibility?

Of the many books on ethics that I have read, none of them would provide a leader with a firm direction on these questions. Leaders need a solid understanding of how to handle ethical questions on a day-to-day basis. Most ethics books provide a wide array of potential approaches to this problem. Very few (none, if I remember correctly) give a process through which someone can work their way to an answer that fits the situation, stakeholders, and belief structures. Narrative Leadership moves into this vacuum with a process and metrics. Because of the complexity of the subject, this book can only outline the approach. More details on the process and metrics will be given in later books and courses. I've tried to supply enough of the details here so that you will have solid and useful information that you can put into practice.

Every action has a value. Actions move us towards or away from something. Actions answer some questions and at the same time ignore other questions. Actions are good or bad, but in the larger scheme of things, never truly indifferent. Actions have consequences that affect our world and thereby change our world.

Several Quick Example

Something as simple as eating breakfast has value judgments when viewed from certain angles. What we eat affects our bodies and our health. How the food was grown or raised has an effect upon our ecology and society. Our choices affect the livelihoods of ranchers, farmers, processors, and retailers. We may decide to ignore these questions, but that doesn't make the effects go away.

Since our foundational narrative drives our actions, foundational narratives are inherently value laden. For example, part of my foundational narrative is that I enjoy being with people, I'm an extrovert. On the surface this may seem neutral, of no ethical issue. But if this were combined with a mean spirit or a desire to be "better than others" this part of my foundational narrative would have a significant negative consequence. Conversely, my extroversion coupled with my desire to leave the world a better place has significant positive consequences for my friends, family, and community. This ethical decision requires that I (at least try to) be aware of the narratives in every contact I have with others.

For those who choose to be friends, parents, or leaders the effect of their foundational narrative becomes significantly greater than if they had not chosen the path of a leader. As leaders some may want to see the work of leadership as "just business." This allows her to limit the questions she has to answer. She can then ignore the emotional or personal results of her decisions. Just because she choose to ignore these issues doesn't mean that her decisions don't have these effects. On the other hand, if she decided to try to analyze all of the effects of any single decision she could spend her whole life analyzing one single decision. This is part of the reason why humans have developed a foundational narrative: it allows us to simplify our life by having a story upon which we base our decisions (rather than having to analyze every action, every single time we make a decision).

The problem is that our foundational narrative has developed slowly over the course of our life. Few of us have ever inspected our foundational narrative to see whether or not it brings out the best in ourselves and helps create the world of our dreams.

One of my neighbors is a good example of this. He believes himself to be a very ethical man. Overall, that is probably true, but he has an anger problem. His anger flows out into the world and darkens the days of most everyone he touches. Knowing my neighbor, I know that an angry world is not the world of his dreams. But because he has not looked at this part of his foundational narrative he has limited his effectiveness as an ethical leader.

One of the characteristics of an ethical leader is that she periodically inspects her own foundational narrative to see if it is helping to create her desired world.

Trust & Leadership

Trust: *Understanding the foundational narrative of another person or organization.*

By this definition, we can trust sharks to act like sharks and Narrative Leaders to act ethically. We can have a level of trust for each of these types of people as long as we have an understanding of how they make decisions. This definition enables the creation of fairly objective measurements of trust. See the section ""Measuring Foundational Narratives (Surprises)," page 161 for more information.

We grow up inside a society in a similar way to how a goldfish grows up inside an aquarium. For the goldfish, the water around them is just part of their life. For the fish to understand how it might be to live in a different aquarium with different water and different plants might be an impossible task. It may be just as difficult for us to understand what it might have been like if we had grown up in a different culture.

For a citizen of the United States, it's difficult to imagine what it might be like to grow up in Bangladesh. Similarly, it's difficult for someone from China to imagine what it would've been like to grow up in Germany. We are a product of our culture. One essential part of each culture is how much it trusts, or doesn't trust, each other, the government, and other societal organizations.

The Pew Global Attitudes Project released a study on how much individuals trust their society and people around them.

Are Most People in Society Trustworthy?

Country	Disagree	Agree
China	19	79
Sweden	22	78
Canada	28	71
Britain	34	65
Egypt	40	58
Indonesia	40	58
United States	41	58
Germany	45	56
Malaysia	42	56
India	45	54
Pakistan	35	54
Jordan	45	52
Venezuela	48	51
Russia	46	50
Mali	51	49
Poland	46	48
Ethiopia	53	47
Ukraine	48	47
Mexico	50	46
South Korea	52	46
Bangladesh	53	45
France	55	45
Ivory Coast	55	45
Bulgaria	48	44
Slovakia	56	43
Spain	54	43
Japan	53	43
Argentina	54	42
South Africa	56	42
Czech Republic	58	42
Israel	56	42
Ghana	56	41
Italy	56	41
Tanzania	56	41
Morocco	44	40
Turkey	55	39
Brazil	65	35
Bolivia	59	35
Palestinian Terr.	58	34
Lebanon	67	33
Senegal	67	32
Nigeria	66	32
Chile	69	29
Uganda	66	29
Peru	69	28
Kuwait	71	27
Kenya	75	25

Figure 4: Pew Research on Trust

The trust level we have for other people deeply affects our personal foundational narrative. Here in the United States we somewhat more trust people than distrust them, while our neighbors to the north, in Canada, greatly trust people more. It can then be expected that if someone grew up in Canada he would probably be more trusting and less protective of himself than if he grew up in the United States or someplace like Kenya.

Therefore, if I'm managing someone who grew up in Kenya, where the distrust is high, I can expect that he would have a strong tendency to distrust me and anything I say. As a leader, it doesn't help to take this personally, because it's not. He grew up in a society that has a strong tendency not to trust.

Let's say I have two people in my group. One is from Kenya and the other from China. If I ask them each to do a task and phrase it in exactly the same way, I can expect two different reactions. The person from China will probably accept my request as prima facie what it seems: a request to do a specific task. On the other hand, the person from Kenya will be much more likely to look at what's behind my request; what does the request imply and what were my motives for asking?

A few years ago I was managing Eric, a man from Kenya. He was bright and I thought had great potential. The company had recently started a fast track training system for people like Eric. I called Eric into my office and asked him if he'd like to join this training. He immediately became furious. After much discussion, I learned that he felt that I was telling him that he wasn't good enough and needed to be "improved." That was not my intention, but, given the society he grew up in it was a quite logical conclusion. His actions (expressed narrative) point towards a foundational narrative that was deeply affected by the general lack of trust in Kenya.

It's not that Eric's foundational narrative was wrong or warped. It was extremely appropriate for the society in which he grew up. If I was managing a division in Kenya the greater level of trust built into my foundational narrative might lead me into many problems. Once again, this brings up the need to understand ourselves as leaders. What are our biases? How, where, and when do we see the world through our own cultural biases? If I'm going to appropriately lead someone like Eric, I need to be able to have some understanding and acceptance for his way of viewing the world. Only then can I give efficient and effective direction that helps individuals and the group achieve our goals.

One option for the leader is to only hire people similar enough to herself that she doesn't have to stretch when leading them. There are two flaws with this thinking:

1) The more similar a group is, the less creative energy that is produced. When dissimilar minds work on a problem, there is a greater potential for more of the important questions to be asked and for innovative answers to be found.

2) When we start to eliminate categories of people from the potential hiring pool, there is no end. The only person who is really like us is ourself. That is, when we want to lead people who are like ourself we are leading a group of one, ourself. In all other cases we are leading a group of varying complexity.

The more dissimilar the group is from each other, the greater the complexity. Because of this complexity, it takes time and attention to lead. Each person has a different foundational narrative, wants to be treated differently, and understands the world differently. When leaders spend great amounts of their time doing technical tasks, there is little time and energy left to perform the difficult tasks of leading.

Trust Example: The NSA & Leakers

I watched the news about the United States National Security Agency (NSA) collecting massive amounts of data. I read how Edward Snowden, the leaker, was a hero or a traitor; how the NSA saved the nation from many catastrophes or how it is an agency totally out of control. Its hard to make sense of the underlying issues given all the noise, rhetoric, and emotion. These types of chaotic times are when a good Narrative Leader can really shine.

The place to start is by understanding the explicit and foundational narratives of the main stakeholders. The whole list of stakeholders includes almost every one in the world e.g: the NSA, the US Federal government, friendly foreign governments, unfriendly foreign governments, people whose records are being scanned, and of course Mr. Snowden. But for starters, the short list would be: Mr. Snowden, the NSA, and the US Federal government.

Even with just a quick narrative analysis, the main issue stands out: trust.

Few outside of the NSA have much knowledge about the expressed narratives, much less the foundational narrative, of the NSA. The NSA's non-verbal expressed narrative is secrecy. From past behavior, they can be expected to act secretly in the future. This gives us some insight into their foundational narrative: "If at all possible, act secretly." Even if many people do not feel comfortable with this narrative, there can be some trust that the NSA will act out this narrative.

Therefore, there can be no narrative positive trust of the organization. (In narrative terms, you can only have positive trust for those who act as you expect them to and therefore you understand to some extent).

> ***Positive trust***: *Where there is both an understanding of another person's, or an organization's foundational narrative and it overlaps with your own.*
>
> ***Negative trust:*** *Where there is an understanding of another person's, or an organization's foundational narrative and it violates the principle or ethic inherent in your own foundational narrative.*

Since all we have from the NSA is secrecy, there is very little we can know about its foundational narrative. We could make up stories about what the NSA's foundational narrative might be and then place our trust in that mirage. Or, we could say that the foundational narrative must be good because we trust the good people leading it.

> ***Referred trust***: *Granting of trust because a person or organization that is the intermediary, is trusted.*
>
> ***Direct trust***: *Granting of trust because the person giving the trust has a personal understanding of the foundational narrative of the person or organization being trusted.*

In Narrative Leadership terms, there can be no real trust between the NSA and the electorate of this country. There may be referred trust, but not direct trust. Where the Federal government and the NSA are making basic errors is in trying to establish a form of trust. These tools are only available to them as a chimera or as referred trust. The government can make up stories that some people will believe for a while. But this falls into the Abraham Lincoln saying "You can fool some of the people all of the time, or all of the people some of the time, but you can not fool all of the people all of the time."

The story the US Federal government tells may be true, but it is unverifiable by the electorate and therefore not a source for wide acceptance and trust. The electorate can more easily understand Mr. Snowden than the NSA. Mr. Snowden is a person, the NSA is a big black box of an organization. If it becomes a battle for trust, it could be very ugly.

There are ways for groups to operate without direct trust. Sometimes it may be necessary, such as in spy organizations. But the organization shouldn't fool itself into thinking that it will have direct trust. There are just too many unknowns. Whatever is said will be interpreted as a falsehood by some of the people, much of the time.

There are two (and possibly more) ways to operate without trust:

1) Referred trust - For example, appoint someone as the head of the organization that is highly trusted by all (especially by opponents).
2) The logical placement of safeguards. That is, hear out all the concerns. Place mutually agreed upon checkpoints or safeguards at each major issue area.

Implementing one of these alternatives to direct trust could be a huge benefit to the NSA:
- More light being shone upon areas ripe for abuse
- More trust from the electorate and foreign governments

- Not creating a system where law abiding citizens turn to encryption and other methods of obscuring their contacts (and thus making it harder to find the terrorists)
- Slowing down the arms race for more cyber-weapons.

The more similar to us an organization is, the easier it is for us to trust it. Three main factors affect our view of how much like us an organization is: **size**, **ethics**, and **expressed narrative**. For size, humans can generally relate more to small organizations than they can to large ones. We tend to trust small ones more than large ones like governments and multinational organizations. The second item, ethics, is a powerful issue. If any organization goes against our ethics, it will be hard for that organization to win back our trust. Mostly, ethics works against organizations rather than for the organization. That is, we rarely know if an organization's ethics line up with ours. It's difficult to know all of an organization's ethics. But when an organization violates our ethics it's a big deal. The third item, expressed narrative, is about how much we like what the organization says, or does, with its products and services.

The NSA is huge, so its size it counts against it. The NSA's ethics appear to differ significantly from the general populace (or at least their ethics differ from what we want it to be). The third main factor, expressed narratives, is problematic for the NSA also. One of its often-repeated expressed narratives is: "Just trust us. We know what we're doing." The NSA has the previous two issues going against it, and this expressed narrative gives us nothing concrete to help us change our distrust.

Trust makes leadership so much easier. But there are situations where referred trust or no trust must be handled. An example is when someone comes into a group as the new manager. There may be referred trust indirectly through the upper level bosses, or from the previous leader. But even more likely is that this new manager will be faced with a situation where there is a referred lack of trust. That is, prior situations color the group's expectations – they are led to expect a less than optimal new situation.

One of the main values of Narrative Leadership is the ability to clearly understand these different trust narratives.

Respect & Leadership

The dictionary definition for respect is one that could lead to a never-ending definition circle: "Esteem for or a sense of the worth or excellence of a person" [dictionary.com]. While their definition of esteem is "Regard with respect or admiration." Round and round we go, with no real help for leaders. This definition of respect doesn't help leaders understand why they are, or are not, respected and doesn't point to what they could do about it. A Narrative Leadership definition of respect is:

> ***Respect****: A person's regard for a person or organization whose foundational narrative strives towards a higher purpose.*

Since our definition of narratives is all from the viewpoint of the narrator, the definitions of "striving" and "higher purpose" are all from the viewpoint of the one who respects, or doesn't respect. That is, if I'm a group leader and wondering why I'm not respected more, I need to look at the foundational narratives of the people I lead and how they view "higher purpose." It doesn't matter that I feel I am doing my absolute best towards a higher purpose, the people I lead may not value that purpose. If they don't, my striving towards this goal doesn't add to their respect for me. As an example:

I'm a Rabbi and I strive towards making this world a better place for everybody. This includes the very simple and minor act of putting a bumper sticker on my car that says: "God bless everyone, no exceptions." A little while ago a man approached me who had great exception to my bumper sticker. He didn't feel that we should bless our enemies. My bumper sticker did not increase his respect for me. What I thought of as a step towards my higher purpose in his view was a step down a wrong path.

In a previous section the definition of trust was given as: "Understanding the foundational narrative of another person or organization." This merges nicely with the above definition of respect. There can be no respect without at least a modicum of trust. That is, we must have some understanding of the individual's foundational narrative in order for us to decide whether or not they are striving towards a higher purpose.

To increase other's respect for you, concentrate on increasing their understanding of your foundational narrative (and thus, building trust). Be more transparent about who you really are. Help people understand the higher goals that your actions and decisions are aiming towards.

Unlike trust, which can be positive or negative (see "Trust & Leadership," page 77), respect, if present, is only positive. The common idea of disrespect is really just the condition where there is no respect coupled with rudeness or disdain. Sometimes leaders get angry when faced with someone who does not respect them. The leader may try to force a display of pseudo-respect, i.e. to act as if the respected was present.

This pseudo-respect is just about worthless as a leadership tool. It does not buy loyalty. As soon as the other person feels safe she will probably leave the group or help get rid of the leader who forced this pseudo-respect. Pseudo-respect is a thin veneer. In addition, pseudo-respect generally undermines positive trust, i.e. it enhances fear and loathing.

> *Respect can be increased by helping people see why you lead, how you lead, and what you value.*

Know What You Don't Know

One of the prime characteristics of a good leader is to know the limits of his knowledge. That is, to know know what they don't know.

Often, we become leaders because of our expertise in one area. As a leader, our span of control is vastly increased. We are asked questions on a wide variety of topics. These questions and their answers can be divided into four categories:

1) Questions that we **think we know** the answer to and we **actually do** know the answer.
2) Questions that we **think we know** the answer to and we **actually don't** know the answer.
3) Questions that we **don't think we know** the answer to but we **actually do** know the answer.
4) Questions that we **don't think we know** the answer to and we **actually don't** know the answer.

In case number one somebody asks a question and we answer correctly. No problem. The person either takes our advice or doesn't.

In case number three somebody asks a question and we dodge the question or refer them to someone else. No problem. We have not led the person astray. We haven't helped either, and we might've been able to.

Case number four is almost the same as case number three. We have not led the person astray and we haven't helped either because we really don't know the answer.

The real problem comes in case number two: somebody asks a question and we supply an answer out of thin air. We HAVE led the person astray. There is potential damage in the following areas:

- The project is harmed or delayed because of the misinformation.
- The relationship with the questioner and their respect for you is damaged.

As this happens more times, the relationship with the group and their respect for you as their leader is damaged. If this becomes a repeated pattern, you lose the honor and respect of the group and are no longer the implicit leader (see "Explicit & Implicit Leadership," page 27). You may still be the explicit leader by the fact that you are the appointed manager, but you have lost that glow of implicit leadership. No longer are people following you because they want to, but because they have to.

The "glow of implicit leadership" is THE single biggest tool in a leader's equipment bag. Without this glow, it's like playing baseball and not having a mitt. You can still play, but it's painful.

It's in our own best interest to understand the boundaries of our knowledge. The smarter you are or the more educated you are, the harder this becomes. There are many times that I honestly think I know an answer because it feels like I know the answer. I've been in school for many decades. In school I was rewarded for good guesses. I've been trained to know the feeling when I have an answer.

As a leader, guessing wrong has an impact many times that of guessing right. In school if we guess wrong we get a little lower grade. As a leader when we guess wrong, we can lose our implicit leadership position. In school I got gold stars, good grades, and praise when I answered correctly. I was mostly ignored when I didn't raise my hand – didn't think that I knew the answer. In school, I was never rewarded for knowing the limits of my knowledge.

Knowing what we don't know takes time to look inward, the willingness to face the desires of our ego, and the honesty to listen to the small, quiet voice of our not knowing. Do whatever it is you need to do to harbor the glow of implicit leadership. Personally, when I am in my better self, I provide at least two provisos for every answer I give for which I am not sure. I outline the areas that I might be wrong: memory, not all the facts, my biases on the subject, not enough time to fully process the information, others may look at the situation differently, etc. [This is all to my wife's exasperation "Yeah, yeah. I know that you're not absolutely positive, but what is it you want to say?"]. I've done it for so long, it's now a habit.

As humans, we will err. Leaders are not immune to this. Sometimes we will err on the side of too much caution (we think we do not know, but we actually do know). Sometimes we will err on the side of too much boldness (we think we do know, but we actually do not know). As in a baseball game, we move around in the field. Sometimes it feels like we are in the right spot, and sometimes not. A good leader learns how to play the game with grace and how to take proper care of the tools of the trade.

> *Know what you don't know. Protect the golden glow of implicit leadership.*

The Narrative of Ethics

> **Ethics**: *A part of the foundational narrative to which the person or organization ascribes value.*

Most organizations and most people ascribe significant value to money. But we rarely hear about the ethic of money. It affects almost every decision an organization makes. Therefore, a good leader will openly talk about it. What's fascinating to me is that in Western society we view money as both an evil and as a highly positive ethic. Rich people have somehow "made it." Many people envy others who have wealth. Since society has the dualistic view of money, most organizations keep salaries a secret. In fact I've been in companies in which it's part of the human resource rules that you are not allowed to tell anybody else how much you make. The ethic in these organizations is in hiding what it values and who it values. We value wealth (the capitalistic ethic) and we value keeping this information quiet (the secrecy ethic).

An ethic is not an absolute, it's a continuum. On one end of the scale are things that are good ideas. These good ideas can be laid aside depending upon the context. For example, I once worked for a company who had a "good idea ethic" of telling customers the whole truth about the equipment. We frequently spent hours discussing with the customer's engineers some of the "back bends" that they'd have to do to get the most out of our equipment. But if the salesperson thought that it might lose the sale, the company would omit detailing some of these issues about our equipment. Money was valued more than telling the whole truth.

At the other end of the ethical values scale are the values that have been battle-hardened. When a conflict of values arises in life, we choose some values over others. Those values that we consistently choose are called our diamond ethics. In between the diamond ethics and the good idea ethics are the structural ethics. These are values that we think are fundamental to our narrative, but have not yet been tested.

> ***Good idea ethic****: A part of the foundational narrative whose value varies depending upon the context.*
>
> ***Structural ethic****: A part of the foundational narrative to which value is ascribed and, around which the individual or organization has structured their thinking process.*
>
> ***Diamond ethic****: A structural ethic that has been tested multiple times and under great stress against other structural ethics. The diamond ethic is the one(s) that is consistently more valued.*

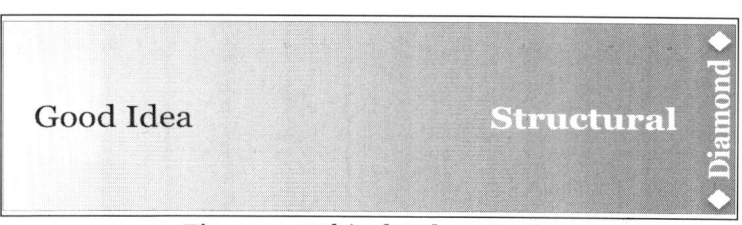

Figure 5: Ethical Values Scale

As an example, parts of my belief in God have been well tested: my belief in the underlying goodness of God is a diamond ethic. Other parts of my belief, such as that God listens to prayer, are structural ethics: I have based my life around prayer and the hope that God listens. In the commonly used sense of the word "ethic," prayer and my belief in God may seem more like belief systems than ethics. But these are value-laden parts of my foundational narrative. Therefore, by the NL definition these are ethics.

There is a good reason for defining ethics in this manner. Firstly, the dictionary definition of ethics, is a fuzzy roundabout kind of thing. Even in the ethics courses I've taken, the term is not well-defined, and the students use it to justify all sorts of actions. Secondly, I wanted to bring it into direct conversation with leaders and into the consciousness of every Narrative Leader. Finally, this definition allows for metrics - ways of measuring the values individuals put on each ethic and how well it integrates into the core narrative.

Elements of Leadership

- Trust
- Respect
- Know what you don't know
- Ethics.

These building blocks are essential to a good leader. They are also essential to a good follower. Knowing who you can trust, when you can trust them, and why you can trust them, makes leading and following so much easier. The three other building blocks support trust and add their own distinct strength to leading and following. When all four are cleanly and clearly interwoven throughout an individual's foundational narrative, the person shines. People are drawn to her. There tends to be a constant, gentle movement towards doing things well, doing things that are for the greatest good, and consideration for all.

The next section discusses how these building blocks of leadership and follower-ship can be discovered in foundational narratives. While reading the next chapter, keep in mind that this is an introductory text. As hinted at in the other sections of the current chapter, there is a tremendous amount of detail available to a trained Narrative Leader. The following chapter is meant to start leaders along the NL path in discovering and uncovering expressed and foundational narratives.

V. Discovering Foundational Narratives

There is truth embedded in all communication. It is the Narrative Leader's journey to discover it.

For Narrative Leaders, the road to understanding foundational narratives is a road of discovery. It is like an archeologist uncovering a civilization, layer by layer. Most of the narrative is not verbalized. For the untrained, it can feel overwhelming to try and analyze another person's foundational narrative. There are short cuts and easier paths to discovery. Some of these are discussed below. Another great path is discussed in the section "Metrics," page 159. Learning how to use these tools takes practice. A mentor experienced in Narrative Leadership can be of immense help. Other options include:

- Talk with your friends and peers.
- Go to the Narrative Leadership website (NarrativeLeadership.info) and enter into the discussion.
- Take some of the courses on the NL website.
- Form a study group with some of your peers.

Professionals, including professional managers, try to continuously improve their craft.

The following methods are meant for use once you are comfortable with the basics of NL and have a good understanding of expressed and foundational narrative. Play with these tools. Notice what you uncover both about foundational narratives and about the tools. Modify these tools to fit your personal style. There is nothing sacrosanct about these tools. They are meant to aid you in your discovery, not get in the way of it.

Using Contextual Clues

Back in the section "Leadership," page 32, I discussed the differences between a clear narrative, a true expression of a person's foundational narrative and a diversion narrative, an expressed narrative meant to divert one from the truth. There are several ways to differentiate these two.

1) Polish. Does the explanation fit a little too well? Foundational narratives are messy things. They are always in the process of being developed. Foundational narratives have lumps, bumps, and scars from life. Real life is not a series of neat little packages.
   - If the explanation is too neatly tied up, it is probably an attempt at misdirection. i.e. a diversion narrative.

2) Tone of voice. Does the tone of voice match what is being said or does it contradict? Is there a significant change in the tone of voice? Examples of tone are pitch, volume, tremors in the voice, harsh or smooth overtones, and pace. Does the tone of voice change when the person enters and exits the explanation?
   - A distinct change in tone usually means that he was either:
     a) Working to construct a new diversion narrative.
     b) Moving from a diversion narrative towards a clear narrative.

3) Body posture. Is she unusually still or fidgety? Does her body movements align with what she is saying or do the movements distract from it? Notice any significant change in her movements.
   - Unless she is a very good actor, it's difficult for anyone to align both her words and her body movements when she does not believe what she says. If her body posture, tone of voice, and words are all in alignment this is likely someone who is speaking from her clear narrative, or at least close to it.

4) Word choice. Does the choice of words fit his normal talking style?
    - Word choice will tend to be more logical, precise, and oddly out of character when he is crafting an expressed narrative.
    - On the other hand, word choice will follow his usual pattern when he is expressing his clear narrative.

Foundational narratives are lumpy, bumpy, living things while diversion narratives tend to be sculpted beauties of persuasion.

For organizations, the contextual clues can generally be lumped into four areas. Through understanding the interplay of these four areas, important issues of the foundational narrative can be more clearly seen:

1) Marketing literature - Who is the organization trying to persuade and why?
    - Marketing literature includes:
        - Literature for customers.
        - Advertisements.
        - Human resource handbooks & guidelines (marketing to employees).
        - News releases.
        - Internal organization-wide memos.
        - White papers & published research papers.
2) General employee environment - Walking through the offices gives a general impression of how management views the employees.
    - How well cared for are the offices?
    - Where is money spent? (Think of top-flight attorney's offices versus an auto mechanic's garage. In a garage, the money is spent on tools, in an attorney's office it's making things plush.)

- What are people doing and how do they sound? (Are they rushed? Are they stressed?...)
- What's on the floor? (Flooring is expensive and lasts a long time. It tells a lot about the foundational narrative. Is it designed to dampen sound, resist spills, take a beating, look institutional...?)

3) Executive environment - How are the executives trying to make themselves different from other employees?
    - Are the executive's doors open or closed?
    - Are the executives in an open floor plan or walled offices?
    - How far are the executive offices from where the work is being done?
    - Which departments are the executive offices near?
    - Do people stop before entering an executive's office or do they just walk in?
    - When executives work outside of their offices, where are they working and at what tasks? How often are they out of their office?

4) Organizational response to problems - What are the coping mechanisms of the organization? These become more obvious when the problem is a crisis, but hints can usually be seen with even the smallest issue.
    - Does the organization try to truly resolve the situation?
    - Who is kept informed and with how much information?
    - Is there a feedback and quality assurance system to ensure that the problem is truly resolved?
    - How quickly is the problem noticed and a problem resolution process started?
    - How quickly do solutions get implemented?

- How quickly is the situation truly resolved?
- Who gets involved in the resolution? How much management oversight is there?
- Who gets involved in the feedback and quality assurance?
- How much angst is involved in problem resolution?

Communication Level

All communication is directed from one entity to another. What the communicator thinks about the receiver is embedded in the communication.

When expressing ourself, we embed in the communication what level we think the the listener is, in relationship to ourself. This communication level can be divided into four categories with regard to the direction from the speaker to the receiver.

***Communication level**: The hierarchy embedded into communication:*

1) ***Up**: Deference. For example: "You might think of it this way" versus "Think of it this way." (The first form contains deference for the listener, and is "Up". The second shows no deference, it is a command - it is definitely not "Up.".)*

2) ***Down**: Superiority. Examples abound: ordering someone to do something rather than asking, snobbery, aloofness, and refusing to answer questions.*

3) ***Even**: Peer. The language tends towards the informal. More frequently a back and forth discussion rather than a monologue.*

4) ***Dialectical***: *In opposition to. Examples include: Us/Them, code words (see below), and technical jargon. Technical jargon might include RAM (computer memory), toroid (a bagel shape), atherosclerosis (hardening of the arteries), and acronyms of all sorts.*

Code word*: A word or phrase used by a subculture or cult that has distinctly different meaning for the subculture than for the larger culture. The purpose of these code words is to differentiate the subculture from the overlying culture and/or to assist the subculture in hiding out in plain sight.*

Examples of code words include: blair (being strong, creative and beautiful), mind of mencia (something so blatantly unfunny that it must have been created in a lab), snecret (a lie by omission), cypherpunk (a guerrilla fighter who is at war for on-line privacy), and typeless (being so astounded that you can't even type. The online equivalent of being speechless). Over time code words may infiltrate the language of the larger culture. Examples of this infiltration include: bagel, ninja, DVD, and cop (as in police).

Assumptive Words

Words that show assumptions can say a great deal about the organization's or person's foundational narrative. Knowing that the person or organization is making these assumptions points directly to how they make decisions. All of life's decisions are made with many assumptions. These assumptions are packaged together with our experiences of the world into our foundational narrative. If we could completely know a person's foundational narrative we would know the assumptions she used in all of her decisions. Likewise, if we knew all of her assumptions, we would understand her foundational narrative. We, as limited human beings, can't have this complete knowledge, therefore we make do with these partial insights into how decisions are made.

One of the main purposes behind NL is to train leaders in how to discover significant portions of an entity's foundational narrative. Understanding an individual's or organization's assumptions can assist a leader in the following ways:

- **Improves communication** - Clear and concise communication can only occur when assumptions are similar between the speaker and the listener. For example, when someone says "A ... B ... C..." you understand that this also includes "x... y... and z...." For example, when I say Americans, am I including illegal residents or citizens that haven't returned to the US in decades? More broadly, am I including people from South America, Central America, and Canada? Depending upon the context, there could make a significant difference in the communication.
- **Defuses tensions** - Helps minimize emotional explosions and, when they do occur, helps get things back on track relatively easily and quickly.
- **Improves planning** - Aids the leader in the planning and communication of plans. When the assumptions are understood, it greatly enhances the likelihood of a positive outcome. This can be especially helpful when approaching one's boss.
- **Leadership** - Is an aid to the leader in understanding group interactions and how to optimize group communications and group work.

Some of the common assumptive words and phrases include:
- **"You know...."** - Generally there is much left out after this phrase.
- **"It's not the way we do it."** - Assumes that the speaker knows the way to do it and the listener doesn't. This may be true, but it is an assumption on the speaker's part until she has checked it out. In addition, a much larger

assumption is that the way she knows is the only way the organization does it, and it is the best way.
- "**....the process...**" - Assumes there is just one process. Also assumes the whole history of that process.
- "**We**" or "**They**" - Assumes a dialectic, "us versus them." Assumes you both agree about who "we" or "they" are.
- "**This ... is ... that.**" - Most definitive declarations contain an amazing number of assumptions. For example: "This book is the best management book that I've ever read." Assumes at least the following:
  - She has read other management books
  - Her rating system for management books
  - Her definition of what constitutes a management book
  - That the listener is interested
  - She actually read the book
  - She remembers clearly the other management she has read.

Assumptive words*: A shortcut verbalization of the foundational narrative revealing biases and attitudes that the speaker does not expressly state. A type of shorthand.*

Assumptive words may show an area in which the speaker has done little introspection. At some point in her life she has accepted the assumptions that underlie these words. There are almost always many reasons why these assumptions were made. Frequently, these assumptions creep into the core narrative. In any case, assumptive words are a significant pointer to the underlying foundational narrative.

Rose-Colored Glasses

It is difficult to see reality if we don't understand ourselves.

We become habituated to the constants in our lives. One of the constants of our life is our own foundational narrative. It is much easier to see other's than our own. We understand the world through our foundational narrative. It is our rose-colored glasses on the world. The problem is that our foundational narrative tints everything we see and understand about reality. For any leader, knowing himself is one of the greatest aids in leading.

I knew a very heartfelt CEO, Carol. Her deep desire was to lead a company that did well and did good. She wanted her employees to feel valued so she devised the compensation plan with many benefits that she knew would be enjoyed. The problem was that she determined what would be enjoyed by others through her own foundational narrative. When she checked out these benefits with some of her employees her body language, tone, and phraseology all came from her foundational narrative. What her employees heard was "This would be a grand package to have wouldn't it?" What she heard was also colored by her foundational narrative. So the feedback she heard was not a true indicator of the feelings of her employees. The way she asked colored their responses and the way she heard colored their replies. When some of the employees left in disgruntlement, she was dismayed and truly didn't understand.

Another example is from one of my startups. There was a certain amount of money that we could allot for each position. We then created a list of items from which people could trade part of their salary for each option they chose. This money was then deducted from the amount paid directly to that person. The list included extra vacation, fully paid health care for the entire family, going to conventions and conferences, a nicer office, and extra stock options. The cost to the company was just the cost of setting up the plan. Essentially, for the company it was cost neutral. Each employee selected the perks that they valued most. I chose extra vacation and extra stock. If I had assumed that everybody else wanted these same perks, some of the employees would have been disgruntled. When setting up the plan, I understood that my way of valuing was not the same as how everyone else would set value. Therefore, I tried to create as large a set of options as the company could easily manage while remaining cost neutral.

The more we understand our foundational narrative and how it might differ from others, the more clearly we can lead. To help understand some of the highlights of your own foundational narrative, it is helpful to watch your reactions in stressful situations.

1) When a "hot button" of yours gets pushed, note where your mind goes.
2) What narrative do you tell yourself?
3) Acknowledge this side-venture to yourself (jot it down, preferably in the moment).
4) Return to listening.
5) Later, review this side-venture with other side ventures your mind has taken in times of stress. What is the pattern? Talking this over with a mentor or friends may be especially helpful. Since, frequently we can't even know we have rose-colored glasses on until someone points it out.

VI. Leadership Styles

There are many leadership styles. Some work well in some situations and terribly in others. No one style that I have yet discovered is useful in all situations. The purpose of this chapter is to:
- list some of the more prevalent styles.
- allow the reader to see parts of their own leadership style and understand more of when and why it works and when and why it doesn't work.
- allow the reader to better see others, and understand how they handle the problems and advantages that these other styles bring.
- be a resource when it becomes obvious that your current leadership style isn't working.
- be an aid when hiring, promoting, or training new leaders.

Each of us has our own unique blend of various leadership styles. Before entering into the discussion of leadership styles, there are two important definitions to keep in mind.

Managing-up*: The art of handling those above you in the hierarchy such that it makes your life easier or better, or makes your work more efficient and effective.*

The art of managing-up is amazing to watch. Some people have a knack for it. Think on the styles listed here as you watch other people manage-up in a way that seems truly effective. As you read these styles of leadership think about how you might manage-up with each one of these styles. Learning this art can greatly assist your career.

Unit of control*: The method or tool that a leader uses to control the speed, direction, and interactions of the group.*

Typical units of control include:
- information

- gathering lots of information
- withholding information
- controlling the flow of information
- feelings
  - warm, good feelings to bind the group together
  - negative feelings about the consequences of failure
  - anger – Some managers purposefully make members of their group angry. People are much easier to control when angry.
- rewards and punishments (more informational than the feelings oriented manager)
- in-group/out-group
  - heroes and goats – Some managers have a particular spin on the in-group/out-group style where you're either a hero of the group or you're a sacrificial goat.
  - winners and losers – Another variant of the in-group/out-group is where managers make work a competition.

Some leaders start with an internal drive to make themselves better (self leadership) and then focusing outwards with the desires to guide and lead others. In others, the leadership drive may not go inward, but remain only as an external focus.

Self-leadership*: The art of looking inward for ways to increase elegance, efficiency, and efficacy (the 3E's), and doing something about it.*

The leadership styles are listed in alphabetical order (except for NL which is given last). Each section has a description of the leadership style, how to recognize the style, when the style is appropriate, and what you can do if this person is a boss, a peer, or an employee.

A short review: When I use the term "manager" or "management," it is a job title that implies a certain amount of authority and responsibility within an organization. Leadership is having a goal and people willingly following you towards that goal.

Proviso: No leadership style works all the time. Each leadership style has its time and place when it works well and is appropriate. Very few people are just one style. Most are a combination of several styles, with one being dominant.

Authoritarian Leader

The authoritarian style of leadership is, perhaps, the one that most of us equate with management. For those over 55, it's the style our parents used when we were small, our teachers used in school, and our parents tried to use when we were teenagers. Maybe, because of this early exposure, authority and responsibility is equated with an authoritarian approach to leadership.

Authoritarian leaders give orders. Feedback is rarely welcome and questions tolerated only when they elucidate the order (and not the order itself. Authoritarian leaders do not welcome anything that might question their authority). There are timelines, rules, and penalties.

Authoritarian leadership is appropriate when lives are at stake. For example when a child is going to touch a hot stove, there's a fire in the building, or a nuclear technician is about to dump the coolant water from a nuclear reactor. These are situations that require fast and decisive action.

This style works on a momentary basis or when people become deeply committed to a cause and mono-focused upon that cause. When overused, authoritarian leadership undermines respect for those with authority and responsibility, and decreases organizational creativity. In addition, this mode of leadership does not work well with people who habitually test their boundaries, for example teenagers and artists. This leadership style tends to work well when leading those who have little tolerance for ambiguity.

When a manager over-uses authoritarian leadership, frequently the implicit leader of the group will emerge. This may be an administrative assistant, a lead person, or the janitor. This is the person who smooths over ruffled feathers so that the real work can get done. If you are a second level manager or executive, watch for these true leaders. They may be causing problems temporarily, because they don't like the way they are being treated. But these are the people who have a natural feel for leadership.

One of the redeeming qualities of authoritarian leadership is that it makes it easier to pinpoint the true leaders within a group.

I have uncovered two separate foundational narratives that drive authoritarian leaders. One revolves around control and the other around power. You may remember that a foundational narrative is a story with a past, present, and future that drives behaviors and decisions. Therefore, you can tell which of these narratives is primary by watching a leader's decisions and behaviors, not what they say.

An authoritarian leader whose foundational narrative centers on control will use their authority to place bounds upon people and tasks. For example, I knew this one authoritarian leader, Marge. Marge would require her group to be in exactly by 8 AM and leave no sooner than 5 PM. She would allow the employees to do their work but would not let them get too far ahead without having their work checked. She was very nice about it, but set very strong limits upon how far people could go, when they could do their work, what work they could do, and when they could do it.

I knew Marge extremely well, and she seems to typify the control-oriented authoritarian managers that I have known. Marge had a need to control. It did not matter what, how big or how small, how important or how mundane. It's not that she would control everything at once and its also not that she didn't know the difference between important and urgent. She just needed to always be controlling something. If no big or important tasks were there to control, she would choose a more minor task or some individual to control.

The truth is, Marge was a fairly effective manager – she got things done. She just was not efficient – a lot of her group's energy was wasted by her controlling the wrong things at the wrong time.

Also, she was not elegant - she irritated most of the group most of the time.

Marge's style of management might feel like micromanaging, but the underlying foundational narrative is entirely different, and therefore needs to be handled quite differently. The way to tell the difference is that the micromanager is oriented around the technical details of the job while a control oriented authoritarian leader is oriented towards placing boundaries.

If you are working for a person like Marge, the primary thing to remember is that it is not about you. It is their issue, and they have a basic need to control. Therefore, give them things to control while giving you space to breathe. For example, Marge and I were supposed to write a book together. So I negotiated with her that she would dictate the timelines and the overall look and feel while I would be in charge of the content. This allowed her to control the issues that worked well with control, and left me free to do my writing, research, breathing, and living.

The other type of authoritarian manager is one whose core narrative has a need for power. Generally, when these people assert their authority its more about people than tasks. They will try to move powerful people under them or into positions that greatly reduce the other person's power. I have known a lot of people like this. For the example Mark, the manager. Mark could not abide people in his groups getting public acclaim. This is typical of this type of manager. They view power as being a zero sum game. A zero sum game is where, if one person wins, another person must lose by the exact same amount. They view the world as either "I win you lose"/"I lose you win." Since they do not want to be on the losing end, they are always on the lookout for who has power and how they can get it from them.

It is not that Mark was a suck up; but if that is what it took to get more power from his boss, that is what Mark would do. On the other hand, Mark would rather have gotten rid of his boss if his boss's power could then come to himself.

When working for a boss like Mark it's important to understand that they can be nice people and okay managers if they can be convinced that this will increase their power. In addition, power oriented managers tend to be future oriented. So, if you can paint them a picture that shows how much they could gain in the future by being a good manager to you in the present, it's likely that they will attempt to be a good manager for you.

Another important issue is that the drive for power generally comes from the core part of their foundational narrative, not the adaptive part. Therefore, it is unlikely that a power-oriented authoritarian leader will easily or quickly change their leadership style.

To sum up, there are two foundational narratives of authoritarian leaders. One is about control while the other is about power. In either case, when managing-up, assist them to feel like they get what they want (control/power) while building strong boundaries within which you can work. Think of it as building strong walls that help keep you safe and your manager's compulsions at bay.

If you're working for an authoritarian manager, and this style doesn't work well for you, I'll offer a few words of solace and some suggestions. Most people don't know how to do things any differently. If they truly understood their effect upon others they would probably do it differently (but the one to point this out will probably be considered an enemy). Most authoritarian managers are aiming towards a goal. If you can understand that goal and help them achieve it, your life as an employee may be easier. In addition, it's a great proving ground to find out your own behind-the-scenes leadership style.

If you are a peer of an authoritarian manager, they will probably, mostly, leave you alone. They might even become good friends. It's difficult for a peer to influence an authoritarian manager. Their focus is mostly oriented up and down the hierarchy. It can be done, but it takes time and care. If you want to help them become a better leader suggest they study someone above them in the hierarchy that you consider to be a good leader.

If someone in your group has an authoritarian narrative, you, as their leader, can probably significantly impact how they view leadership and management. They may be slow to change or it might take a significant impact for them to change. The change can be accelerated by having good metrics to measure their progress.

Bossy-Boss

When I think of a bossy-boss, I think of my corgi dog. Corgis are herding animals, and they bark a lot. The bossy-boss can be recognized because they rarely let a decision be made without their voice being heard ("bark bark bark... bark, bark").

Bossy-bosses have a need to feel involved. Frequently this comes across as ordering people around. Sometimes it seems like everywhere you turn, there is your boss. The underlying foundational narrative tends to come from one of two foundational narratives:

- A gaping sense that he doesn't really matter. He then overcompensates by trying to be indispensable.
- A lack of understanding of what a leader is. Therefore he has built up a story that the leader is "the decider."

The essence of both of these cases is that the person does not have a well-grounded foundational narrative of what a leader is. Leadership-wise, this person is too immature to be in a leadership position. For some people, leadership does not match their foundational narrative. Other people may not have had a model for what a leader is. And a few others, may eventually mature into leaders.

What this style does is to force the group to work around the manager. On rare occasions, this actually might be a good thing. For example, if your group is stuck and can't find a creative way out of their position, this style of leadership may actually help. In almost every other case, this leadership style is a drag on the organization.

If you're working for a bossy-boss your best bet is probably to show them a model of leadership that works. Bossy-bosses may have an even more fragile ego about their ability to do their job than most other managers. So you'll probably have to approach them obliquely. Find great articles for them to read and tell them how much you enjoyed this article and how it reminded you of them (you need not say that the reminder was in the absence rather than the existence). Urge them to go to a movie with you that has a good leadership model in it. Or just rave about the picture and the leader. Help them see options. Help them see what is excellence. Always keep in mind the fragile ego that underlies this style.

If this person is a peer of yours, they may be open to mentorship. Give them books and articles that helped you become the leader that you are. Invite them to talk about leadership over lunch. Start a leadership support group. It may add more work onto you, but the payoff for the organization is large. Also, others may notice how your leadership extends beyond your own group.

If the bossy-boss works for you, you have three choices:

1) Let them learn on the job. This will probably create high turnover within the group and the group's efficiency is going to suffer.

2) Move them out of the job. The group will be grateful but the manager's ego is going to take a big hit. Their ego is already fragile and it's likely that they will leave. If they don't leave, their efficiency may take a hit and they may try and spread dissent.

3) Teach them what it takes to be a leader. This will take time and attention. Meanwhile the group may be falling apart and its efficiency is probably suffering.

None of these options is particularly desirable. But if handled correctly, options two and three can work well. It takes understanding the individual's foundational narrative around leadership and their leadership ethic (see "The Narrative of Ethics," page 88). My suggestion is to wait for a teachable moment.

> ***Teachable moment***: *A relatively short period of time where an individual's or an organization's foundational narrative is undergoing a structural change and is open to outside suggestions. This usually occurs after a shock to the system. In more aware individuals this can occur when they feel that their current foundational narrative won't get them to where they want to be.*

Drama King/Queen

In general, I enjoy watching leaders do their thing. But the drama King/Queen style is the one I enjoy the most. He can be fun if he realizes that he is a drama addict and learns to play with it. "Addict" might be a little bit strong of a word but for him this style has become much more than a desire or even a habit.

A drama King throws himself into his life with amazing intensity. The emotions of the moment spread out over all their communications and all the people they contact. When in full swing he is like an actor upon the stage of life, fully engaged with his persona of the moment. When enjoying himself he can knit together a group stronger than any other leadership style. If he is in a fairly consistent bad mood, he can destroy not only his own group's morale, but also many of the groups with which he has contact. Frequently, his unit of control is his feelings. He leads people to excellence by inspiring them with joy and excitement. He also can destroy a group by his excellent emotional communication skills when he is in despair.

When used positively, this leadership style can inspire many innovations. The positive use of good feelings can be overused. If you use this style, watch carefully for burnout within your group. Well before anyone is burned out, either switch styles or switch into the neutral dramatic mode (that is, still be you, but keep tight control on your emotional communication).

If this person is your boss, enjoy the high notes and protect yourself from the low notes. There are many ways of protecting yourself from the low notes of his emotions. Some ways include: taking vacation, realizing that this too shall pass, make light of it with him (but never make fun of him), exercise it out of your system, or meditation. In addition, watch for your own burnout both in the high times and in the low times. As you approach burnout a temporary change of scenery is probably required.

If this person is your peer, look for ways of protecting your group from the low notes while still allowing them to revel in the high notes. For you personally, see if you can enjoy playing with his drama. Drama Kings frequently love to have a drama partner. It can defuse the negative emotional impacts and the strong negative self talk he frequently has.

As an employee, the drama King can be a fun, exciting, and an innovative handful to manage. If he has not yet learned how to play with his drama, helping him to do so will greatly help moderate the lows. Maybe, play with him in his drama. Directing him when he's in his high notes is as simple as writing out a general script for where he is to go, when he should be done, and maybe a challenge or two thrown in. When he is in his low notes, he may need assistance in seeing much of a future at all. My experience is that a fair percentage of drama Kings have resorted to drug use if he hasn't found out that this style of his can be quite healthy. He uses the drugs to help through the low notes. If you're managing him, watch for drug use and help him get assistance as early as possible. He can be a valuable employee and probably well worth the effort.

Expert

The Expert and the Know-It-all are closely related expressions leadership styles. Both types need to be right. The expert is quiet about it, while the Know-It-All needs to make sure that people are aware of how much they know. See the section "Know-It-All" on page 116 for more details on that style.

The Expert generally does know a lot so, people are apt to come to them for help. As a resource person this would work fine, but as a leader or manager this can be destructive. One of the purposes of a leader is to build talent within their group. If people rely upon the leader for assistance they are not learning what they need to know to grow in their jobs. The more a group relies upon its leader, the less creative, responsive, and efficient the group is.

The purpose of a leader is to lead, that is, to find the best path towards the group's goals and to create an environment that assists in achieving those goals. This is no easy task. It takes a special kind of person and it takes a lot of time and energy. A good leader makes rough roads seem ordinary and, seemingly impossible climbs feel doable and fun. Bad managers make daily tasks feel arduous and fill the worksite with animosity. The Expert puts their energy into maintaining their expertise rather than into becoming a better leader.

Experts generally rely upon the techniques that got them attention and promotion: their expertise at some technical issue. Leadership is a different animal. If they applied the same energy and attention to learning about leadership they might become an excellent leader, but they would slowly lose their edge in the technology because their main attention went into leadership.

Managers who have the Expert leadership style can be recognized by asking them a highly detailed or edge-of-the-art question. If they answer with great detail, they are the Expert. If they refer you to someone else in the group or ask you to look it up and get back to them, this is probably not someone who has this style.

The Expert style can work with groups that are newly formed or are comprised of people who don't have much experience in the field. This style doesn't work well with more mature groups or more mature people.

One Expert manager, Mike, has the need for everybody to come to him on certain technical issues. Another Expert manager, Mary, feels that detailed knowledge of the technology enhances her ability to lead. Mike's narrative as the Expert includes a modicum of control. Mary's narrative started off as a healthy leadership style but fell into error when she started to spend valuable time and resources on maintaining her expertise at the expense of improving her leadership. Both Mike and Mary have a foundational narrative that states, "I don't know how to lead but I do know how to be an expert." Therefore they do what is comfortable, rather than what is needed.

If you're working for an Expert you can explain to them that you need to learn the technology for yourself. This won't make them a better manager but it might make you a better employee. The underlying issue when trying to manage-up (manage your manager) is that your manager is stuck. They can move forward in what their job was, but not at what it is. These Experts tend to be good at many things, so learn from them. Sometimes you can befriend them and possibly help them grow.

Almost all new managers use the Expert style. If you are their boss, it's your responsibility to help them grow. Get them to understand that the first part of leadership is about building the capabilities of the group. It may take them a while to fully understand the complexities of leadership since they may not have had many models of good leadership.

If the Expert is your peer, you may be able to help them grow. But it is also likely that they will be highly guarded in this regard. They are used to being better at their job than any of their peers. So learning from a peer may be difficult. On the other hand, Experts generally will love to learn new technology. So if leadership is couched as a new technology, they may welcome the new information.

Fear-Based Leadership

I have known a few fear-based managers, one quite well. These managers used fear as their tool to control others. Fear was not the endgame but the tool to get what they wanted.

For people who choose the fear-based style of leadership, it is generally not terror that they wish to induce, just enough fear or unease to move others in the desired direction. Frequently it is an implicit message, something like "If you do not do what I want, I will make sure that you regret it."

Fear-based management is easy to recognize: the stick is used far more often than the carrot. That is, rarely do fear-based managers use rewards to motivate their staff.

This is one of the appropriate styles to use when a group has become stuck and other methods of motivation have not worked. On rare occasions I have used this style. I have used it when an employee has worked himself up to an emotional furor and talking him down has not worked. Then, I will bring out this big gun, and put it away quickly when he has calmed down enough to listen. Note that this is a destructive form of leadership. Its use is when an employee or a group has built themselves a fortress from which you have not been able to lead them out. It happens sometimes. People get triggered so that their walls go up and they stop listening.

This style of management is extremely destructive when used with people who are sensitive, very creative, or have a fragile sense of self. It can move these people out of being creative and efficient to being stuck and angry. In addition, some people react to fear with anger. This can take the form of physical or verbal fighting and other inappropriate modes showing their anger.

If you are working for a fear-based manager it can be extremely rough on the ego. First, realize that it is not about you but about the manager. Second, is that the use of fear is about control. They want control in their life and not necessarily control of you.

What I have found works is to give them control over the immediate issue and then start talking to them, on a friendly basis, about general principles or directions. ("Yes, I will do it your way. I apologize for being so bullheaded that you felt you had to threaten to fire me. Maybe, at another time, we can talk about ways to get me to do the work your way without having to threaten to fire me.") Then, as the next situation starts to heat up I gently remind them of the fear induction they used the last time ("Remember last time you implied you might fire me?"). This generally defuses the immediate issue and reminds them of their own anger problem. This method takes forethought and self-control, neither of which you may have in the heat of the situation. Therefore, my suggestion is to start thinking about the directions you want to go and the control issues that you want to defuse, at a time when things are not so stressful.

If you are working alongside a fear-based manager, the natural reaction is to distance yourself from that person. This is partly because these managers' control issues are not solely directed downwards but towards everyone around them. A natural reaction is to give these people what they want, but this is damaging for the organization. Fear-based managers can warp the foundational narrative of the organization. The organization can quickly change to one of control and punishment. It is easy to say that standing up firmly to these fear-based managers is good for the organization. It is much harder to do this in the heat of the situation. In general, standing up to these people early and often (especially on small issues) can get them to focus their energies elsewhere. Rarely will a fear-based manager go into an escalating spiral with peers. Generally, they know fear so well that they are themselves afraid that they might lose the battle. For fear based managers, losing one big battle is like losing the war in which they envision themselves.

If a fear-based manager is working for you, it is important to realize the damage that this leadership style can do. My experience is that generally fear-based leaders are intelligent, but spoiled. Retraining them is a bit like retraining a teenager. Expect tantrums and reversions to old behaviors. But like teenagers, if and when they grow up they can be quite productive members of society. Because their emotional growth is much like that of a teenager, treating them too harshly or trying to move them too quickly can result in them picking up their marbles and going somewhere else to play (i.e. quitting). But, for the sake of the organization and the group that they lead, firm boundaries need to be placed upon them so that they do not continue to do harm.

His/Her Highness

There are many people whose narrative is that leadership sets them above the people they lead. In her worldview, goodness and retribution rain down from above with a swish of her magic wand. She controls the goodness and she directs the retribution. "Her people" are her subjects. She may not know more than others in the group, she doesn't have to. She is the ruler of her minuscule domain.

Her highness's foundational narrative around leadership is that being a leader has value in itself. The title "manager" or "executive" is a crown that shows her value as a human being. She likes others to know how high in the hierarchy she is. It's more than feeling good about having attained the position. That's a normal part of being human. It's that the position itself has value. It's not how good of a leader she is, it's that she has this position.

One manager, Marcia, was particularly bothered when someone in her group wrote a letter to a customer. Nowhere in the letter did it mention that this was Marcia's group. She was really upset, and demanded that in the future that whenever a letter came from this group to a customer, that the group's name and its manager be mentioned. Something like: "Curriculum Development Group, Marcia Mayhem, Manager."

To some, it may seem like just childish ego. But to Her Highness this is an acknowledgment of the hierarchy. A refusal to play the game is, in Her Highness's mind, the same as denying that the hierarchy exists.

These people tend to love to hand out business cards, introduce themselves by their job title, tend to dress appropriate to the royal position, and distance themselves from their underlings. His Royal Highness is easy to spot if you are aware of this style.

This form of leadership can be useful when one of your group is attempting to usurp your position. If overused, this leadership style creates animosity. Therefore, if you do elect to use this leadership style, taper off on its use as soon as practicable.

If Her Highness is your boss, her demands for your obeisance may seem strange or misplaced. A normal response is to resist her requests. This will only make her requests stronger and more frequent. Paradoxically, the way to get her to back off is to give her what she wants at times when she's not asking for it. For example, Her Highness demands that you add her name to any correspondence with customers. Then, as her name in position to any internal email and memos were you are acting as a member of the group. Giving her what she wants, and more so can significantly decrease the number of obeisances she requests of you.

As a peer or her boss, Her Highness is generally pretty easy to get along with. Usually, Her Highness makes few royal demands of her peers or her boss. If you notice her royal behavior, occasionally talking to her about the downside of this behavior can help her grow out of this behavior.

Know-It-All

The know-it-all is an extroverted nerd with more ego. Nerds can be pretty easy to put up with; she knows she can figure out the answer and she will. Know-it-all's will tell you all about it, both before he gets the assignment and after he has completed it. Some know-it-all's have an internal wisdom that he may fail, but he will rarely let you see it. Other's haven't yet gained that wisdom. In either case, his cocksure attitude may feel irritating.

The nerd and the know-it-all are both great for doing research. The nerd tends to come out of a joy of the research itself while the know-it-all may be doing it out of a fear of failure. Since the know-it-all is afraid of failure, he can tie himself up with fear. His feeding and care include controlling the expressions of his ego and easing his fear. Unlike the nerd, when he fails it can be disastrous, he may try to hide it, blame it on someone else, or go into a spiral of self loathing.

There are many similarities between the know-it-all and the narcissist. One of the main differences is that the know-it-all's unit of control is information while the narcissist's unit of control is feelings.

You can spot him quite easily, because he will tell you that he does know it all, or if he doesn't know it now, he will. The know-it-all will rarely be silent throughout a meeting. He likes to be heard, after all he is an extrovert.

If your boss is a know-it-all, it may help to know that there is, probably, a deep fear of failure underneath that façade. Remember that people follow people like your boss because, in general, they do know what they're talking about. He does have a great deal of data at his fingertips. If you can, let the bravado go unheard, and see the excellence that he desires to bring to the group.

If this is one of your peers, you may often feel like screaming at him to be quiet. Realize that his boss probably knows that he is a know-it-all. It's hard to miss. You can gain from him a vast font of knowledge. He may not yet have the wisdom to temper his style, but underneath is a worthy compatriot.

As an employee, someone always tooting their own horn can be greatly irritating. But again, he usually does accomplish what he says he will. It's a mixed bag. It can be helpful to him to gently help him understand how he affects others. He probably wants to be liked and doesn't realize how off-putting this style can be. Giving him public kudos for his accomplishments can be problematic. Group morale can suffer if they see him getting ahead from what they think is self-aggrandizement. In addition his own ego can stoke the fires of his know-it-all-ness.

Laissez-Faire Management

I have never met anyone who is consistently a laissez-faire manager. This is not to say that they're not out there, but most of the managers who use a laissez-faire style of management tend to vacillate between this and another style.

Laissez-faire management is not really a form of leadership. This style is an abdication of authority. This does not abdicate responsibility, that remains with the manager whether they want the responsibility or not. The only way to abdicate responsibility is to step out of the leadership role. What this manager is saying is that she doesn't want to be a leader. The followers of laissez-faire managers have no one leading. It's hard for a group to stay together as a team under this type of manager.

I have deduced four major reasons why people might choose the style of management:

1) A desire to abdicate responsibility – She feels that by not leading she can avoid the aches, pains, and anxiety of leading a group. Frequently a major driver is fear of failure.

2) A desire to abdicate authority – Her foundational narrative has a strong negative emotion around leadership. Frequently a major driver is the fear of being special at the same time very much wanting to be special.

3) A desire to be friends with everyone – Leadership is a lonely position. There are many people who can't stand this loneliness. Some choose this style of management in a desire to be seen as not ordering people around. Her desire to be loved has overcome her desire to lead.

4) Retired-in-place (RIP) – Some people, especially those looking forward to retirement, just don't want to make decisions anymore. She doesn't want to lead, and she doesn't want to manage. The graceful thing for an executive who has a RIP manager is to move her into a staff position, out of direct management responsibilities. The longer she stays in place, the more her group devolves into chaos. (See "Retired-in-place," page 49.)

This is an easy style to recognize: within the group of a laissez-faire manager, either no leader will be apparent or multiple leaders will be struggling for control. No Narrative Leader should allow this to continue for an extended period of time. Laissez-faire management can be an effective way to see who are the real leaders within your group. But if this style is continued for too long, a struggle for leadership can destroy morale.

If you're working for a laissez-faire manager realize that everyone within the group is looking for some leadership. Some personality types deeply desire to have the authority of leadership. Other personality types don't want the responsibility. Watching this struggle within yourself and within others can be immensely instructive. A laissez-faire manager can be really crazy making when he couples this style with an occasional bout of authoritarian leadership. Again, this can be an immensely instructive time. There are almost always clues when a laissez-faire manager is about to switch to another leadership style. This can be used to hone your own understanding of others and yourself. Also, working for a laissez-faire manager can be a very instructive time for learning how to manage-up (see "Leadership Styles," page 101).

Some of the clues that a laissez-faire manager is about to switch styles are when she shows significant signs of:
- irritability
- mental fog or confusion
- overly effusive with emotions
- increased absenteeism
- increased time spent at work, but outside the group.

I have worked alongside a few laissez-faire managers. For me, it's always been frustrating to see how his group struggled to maintain an even keel. In my experience, a laissez-faire manager will readily take suggestions if it makes his job easier. It's all been a matter of determining which suggestions he might accept, and then figuring out how to approach him properly.

If you have a laissez-faire manager working for you, there are three choices:
1) Move the person into a staff position. Then you can utilize the experience and knowledge that he has without allowing harm to come to any group.
2) Accept this individual's limitations along with the damage that he might cause.

3) Require that he step up his game. Have him learn new talents and teach others. This may be very uncomfortable for him, and he may act accordingly. Be prepared.

Loner

The loner is an introvert with a high orientation towards her feelings. She feels deeply but may not be able to express them or show them to others. The loner is generally quiet and, whens she speaks, it is usually well thought through. This is why people follow her. The loner may vary a lot in how much she wants to be alone. The higher the stress, the more alone time she needs. Frequently, the loner is excellent in crisis situations.

This style of leadership can be very useful if you want to build up the group's ability to self-direct. If you use this style, be aware that some personality types may try to help you out of what they see as a funk. They may concentrate more on helping you then doing their job or, perhaps just as a distraction from their job.

Usually, this style of leadership is obvious. If you're unsure, watch how she reacts as the stress builds up. If she tends to go quieter and be more efficient as the stress builds up, then she is probably a loner.

If your boss is a loner, be aware that she probably feels things deeply and keenly. Don't overload her with your emotions, and don't expect her to bare hers. In general, loners expect their group to be self-directed. If this is not your native style, it might be a good time to develop this trait. When times get rough, loners can be excellent leaders to show the group the way out. If you can get her talking about her vision of the future, you might see some tremendous insights.

For many people, working beside a loner can be very trying. It can feel like shouting into a vast empty amphitheater. Be aware though, the loner takes in much more than she lets on. A gentle hand and a soft voice will get you much farther than trying to get a reaction out of her. The loners that I have met all seem to have a harsh inner critic. If you can help the loner see what she does well and how they positively affect other people the returns can be large for the organization.

If an employee of yours is a loner, you're probably glad that she takes so little management time. You may be missing, though, that the feeding and care of a loner requires gentle persuasions towards lightness and joy.

Part of the reason why I have so little to say about the loner is that they are very self-contained. All they need is a sprinkle of joy, a dash of appreciation, and a modicum of understanding.

Micromanager

In general, the micromanager is the scourge of all leaders. In reality, this is not a form of leadership but is a form of management. That is, he is showing his group no leadership, no direction, no model for how to excel, and no encouragement to be better at their jobs. In addition, he actively tears down the self-confidence of the group. This is someone who has attained the perfection of the Peter Principle; he has attained his level of incompetence.

The micromanager is an easy style for people within his group to recognize. It is much harder to recognize from the outside. At this present time, I have only two indicators for those outside to notice:

1) Ask the people within his group what they think of his management style. The group of a micromanager will have a clear view if he uses this style.
2) The number of surprises coming out of this group will probably be high. He is not allowing his group to excel, and they are probably allowing him to fail. For more details see "Measuring Foundational Narratives (Surprises)," page 161.

There may be rare times when this is an appropriate style of leadership. For example, if your group consists of people with little or no training and are too new at work situations to be self driven. In general, avoid this style!

If you're working for a micromanager, you have my sympathy. I have had little success in managing-up with a micromanager. He may be struggling to understand how to move forward as a leader. Alternatively he may be retired-in-place. If you determine that he does desire to grow, you may be able to assist him in seeing the results of his current actions. Frequently, though, this style is mixed with a measure of the authoritarian style. In that case he won't take constructive criticism well.

If one of your peers is the micromanager he may be open to a peer's gentle constructive criticism. My suggestion is to concentrate on what he should be aiming at rather than what he shouldn't be doing. Inform him of the results of his actions, but the concentration is on leading him out of this hole. If he is open to learning, it may take a little time but his group will greatly benefit for it.

As an employee, the micromanager is problematic. He generally doesn't mess up badly enough to fire him; but he destroys the morale and efficiency of his group. Determine if he is RIP or desires to learn. If he wants to grow, devise a series of metrics that measure the amount of micromanagement he is doing and the amount of leadership he is showing. Give him a method of learning that suits his learning style: books, courses, mentoring.

Narcissistic Leadership

I am not equating people who use narcissistic leadership with people who have narcissistic personality disorder (NPD). People with NPD have these traits to an excess that truly disorders their lives. For a narcissistic leader, these traits disorder the organization, but may not be a significant disorder for the individual. If a leader has four or more of the following traits, he is probably a narcissistic leader:

1) Believing that he is better than others.
2) Fantasizing about power, success and attractiveness.
3) Exaggerating his achievements or talents.
4) Expecting constant praise and admiration.
5) Believing that he is special and acting accordingly.

6) Failing to recognize other people's emotions, feelings, and talents.
7) Expecting others to go along with his ideas and plans.
8) Taking advantage of others.
9) Expressing disdain for those he feels are inferior.
10) Being jealous of others.
11) Believing that others are jealous of him.
12) Trouble keeping healthy relationships.
13) Setting unrealistic goals.
14) Easily hurt and rejected.
15) Having a fragile self-esteem.
16) Appearing as tough-minded or unemotional.

Narcissistic leaders may not seem easily hurt or to have a fragile self-esteem, but this underlies all the other traits of this leadership style. In my experience, these leaders **feel** that they are crucial to anything getting done within the group. When they're not around they feel that nothing is getting done, and when they are present they feel that only with their input and direction can the group achieve its goals. Western society tends to value many of the hard-minded traits listed above. Therefore a large number of narcissistic leaders make it into the C-suite.

Narcissists tend to be successful because of their contacts, power, money or their personality (which can be quite enjoyable if you're not working for them). Because they tend to be successful they get little feedback on the damage that this leadership style does.

Narcissistic leadership has its time and place if it is used in extreme moderation. It's when these traits are un-ameliorated by understanding its effect upon others, that problems occur. Each of the above listed traits can be helpful when leading others. These traits become damaging when we take advantage of someone against their will, or through coercion. Some of these traits, when moderated, are a sign of good and appropriate ego development. For example, you may actually be better at your job than others around you and recognizing this is an adult behavior.

When used consciously and in great moderation, this style can be quite helpful when the group has very low self-esteem. A good Narrative Leader could temporarily take on this form of leadership to model for other people what it's like to perform good self-care. The key is not to overdo it.

Sometimes it is hard for upper management to recognize that they have a narcissistic manager working for them. Narcissistic managers make it look like they truly are at the core of anything getting done within the group. They have learned the art of taking recognition for good works and laying blame on others. What's true, is that most of the time narcissistic leaders believe their own hype, that they are better than others, including their boss. The narcissistic leader may try to scramble up and over his boss. Therefore he rarely has long-term friends within upper management circles. A typical scenario is that he got the job through having a friend within the company and that over time the two of them drifted apart and perhaps even became enemies.

If you're working for a narcissistic boss you can try to wait them out or transfer to another group. There is no getting on his good side for more than a moment. If you're helping him get ahead now, you're on his good side for now. If you might take glory away from him, you may be permanently on his bad side. Keeping your head low can work very well. Do your job. Do it well. Don't expect kudos. In his view, the world revolves around him. He leads his group in a way that prevents the world from giving him negative feedback. If the world gives him negative feedback, then the world is wrong.

If you're a peer or boss of a narcissistic leader, safety comes at a cost. A narcissistic leader will use others to get what he wants. Protection from the narcissistic leader's power compulsion comes from enough people understanding that there is a shark in their midst, and appropriate boundaries put upon that person.

If you think you have a narcissistic leader around you, keep things light and friendly with him. He generally does not take well to knowing he has been found out. Remember that he has a very fragile self-esteem.

Nerd

Like the loner, the nerd gets her internal refreshment from being alone. But unlike the loner, the nerd is oriented towards information instead of feelings. She is the quintessential researcher, a walking Wikipedia. People follow the nerd because she is an expert without having the ego of the expert style.

Some nerds are oriented towards a breadth of knowledge, while others are narrowly focused. You'll recognize a nerd if you ask her an obscure question. She will probably pop out with the answer immediately. If not, she will know how to quickly find the answer.

To many non-nerds, she might seem like an impenetrable black box; you ask a question and feed the black box some seemingly unrelated information and out pops an elegant answer. Most nerds can't tell you how she came up with the answer but knew when she was on the right trail. The proper care and feeding of most nerds is recognition, good equipment to work with, and all the information that they desire. Nerds don't tend to be self-appointed leaders except in their field of expertise.

If you work for a nerd, it's much like working for a loner. She expects you to be self-directed and to let her know what you need. Unlike a loner, she can generally handle your emotions. She may not want to, but she can handle it. Nerds like solving problems. If you encounter a problem, don't spend a long time trying to figure it out for yourself. Go to your nerd boss and quickly outline the problem and the solutions you have researched. In general, she will appreciate your not being stuck on one thing for too long.

If your peer is a nerd, she can be a great resource when you have a really hard problem to tackle. Every once in a while, a show of genuine appreciation is welcomed. But, if there is any falseness in the kudos, she will dwell on the falseness and it will be a long time before trust is rebuilt. In general, nerds have a long and useful memory (for things that they deem important).

A nerd employee can be wonderful and joyful to manage until she gets the ego of the expert. It's a careful balance between showing your appreciation and making her think that she is God's gift to your organization. Sometimes it's good to see a nerd fail at a task. The humility that she doesn't know everything can make her a better leader and more cautious in the future. A nerd that hasn't known significant failure may over value her ability to solve any problem presented to her. Therefore, especially with younger nerds, be aware that she may have the belief that her mind can think her out of any problem. Wisdom may come with age and tell her differently.

NO! Leader

There are some people whose first reaction is "No!" I call these people No!Leaders.

The driving force behind this style of leadership is fear. This is the fear of the unknown, fear of change, fear of doing things wrong, and fear of being seen for who he really is. This is quite different from those who use fear as a management tool to control others. For the No!Leader the fear dwells inside of him. Having a glimmer of why he fears so much and how the fear expresses itself can be extremely helpful in working with, managing, or working for the No!Leader.

My experience with working with No!Leaders is that, almost invariably, whenever a suggestion comes up his first words are "No. Because...." It's important to note what follows "Because." Whatever it is, is not his real concern. Usually, it is a blind alley, meant to send the listener off the trail and give the No!Leader time and safety (a diversion narrative). Upon inspection, I've found that for many a No!Leader, what follows the "Because" is entirely made up. Something he grabbed in his panic that sounded or felt true to him, or true enough, that he uses this as his safety net.

If you're the type of person who is not afraid of confrontation and likes to be very straightforward, you might try calling the No!Leader's bluff. It's likely that he will stop, or modify his behavior when working with you. The problem is that this will probably increase his fear when he is around you.

Another potential approach is to give him what he wants, either time or safety. You can tell which it is, or which is more prevalent, by noticing his responses over time. For example some No!Leaders will change their minds, or at least review the issue after a few minutes, a few hours, or a few days. When working with one such leader, I'd say something like "I have an idea that I'd like you to consider, but we don't have time to go into it at the moment. So if you just put it in the back your mind, maybe we can talk about it tomorrow." This person happened to have a 24 hour No!Cycle. Usually he would answer "No" immediately anyways. But I had already set the stage allowing me to come back after the gestation period.

If the person doesn't seem to have a fairly consistent No!Cycle then the fear may be coming from a safety issue. These are frequently the people who call upon "experts" to justify their saying no. The problem with using these experts as the basis for the decision is that when fear is the driver frequently the "expert data" doesn't bear out their conclusions. The more intelligent the leaders are, the more likely that they will have something pertinent to fill in the gap. But in any case, the data, the experts, and the reasons given are all a ruse to hide their fear. This leadership style is the master of the diversion narrative.

I've found that there tend to be two types of fear: 1) the fear of change, and 2) the fear of everything. If it's the former, there are ways to move things to a better footing: show that what you are proposing is a logical extension of where things are today. If it's the fear of everything, it's like a cat on a hot tin roof: everything increases his fear. I've worked with many people like that. What I've done is take them for a walk while we are talking. It's hard for them to freeze up inside when their bodies are in movement.

As a Narrative Leader, you might want to take on this style, temporarily, when you want your people to think deeper before coming to you. Used sparingly, this style can induce creativity. Used too much, creativity can be shattered for quite a while. This style of leadership does not work well when leading people with low self-esteem. They may not have the internal drive to keep coming back with ideas and thoughtful creativity.

If you work for a No!Leader, see if you can get him out of his office when talking. Generally, his office has become part of his stuck place. As mentioned above, see if you can determine his cycle time and use this to your advantage.

If you're working with a No!Leader, see if you can gently point out this pattern of saying "No!" He is probably fear-based, so be gentle and try not to increase his level of discomfort. Most of these leaders don't see their own pattern. Some have convinced themselves that this pattern is actually a good thing.

A No!Leader may be harder to spot if he works for you than if you work for him. His fear likely translates into a fear of saying "No" to you. You may be able to see this leader more clearly by measuring the sparks that come out of his group (see "Measuring The Work Environment for Innovation (Sparks)," page 164). As his manager, it is your job to help him acknowledge his fear and help him to do something constructive about it. In general, this person is not a shrinking violet, so a fairly direct approach may work well. This behavior usually comes out of his adaptive narrative as an reaction to an earlier, very risky environment.

Out-Of-Integrity Leader

The out-of-integrity leader is doing something against her own ethical principles. Frequently these actions have nothing to do with the work itself, but spill over into the work environment. It is not, necessarily, that she is doing something against other people's ethics, it is that she is violating her own principles.

Many out-of-integrity leaders are also sharks. All sharks though, are not out-of-integrity leaders. There are many sharks who believe that what they are doing is acting with integrity. Their ethical system values their actions. On the other hand, an out-of-integrity leader believes that what she is doing is wrong.

There are several indicators for the out-of-integrity leader:
- Makes decisions and does not inform those effected.
- Rather than resolve the underlying issues, she prefers to fix only the presenting problem.
- Avoids confrontation. When attempts at confrontation are made, uses the power of her position to end the confrontation.
- Power is more important than prestige, money, or her good name.
- Frequently can talk clearly about the issues, but decisions are not made based upon the issues at hand but upon unspoken factors.
- Frequently finds ways to sideline or get rid of her best people. These good people (whether they are working for this manager or alongside of this manager) threaten the delicate balance that she has achieved.
- In place of the excellence that threatens her, she promotes less knowledgeable and more manipulatable people who may appear, to outsiders, as "up-and-comers."
- Frequently, the out-of-integrity managers are "nice people" when not in a situation of power. For these unfortunate people, power corrupts absolutely.

If the situation is allowed to continue, the moral standing of the organization will suffer. In addition, the ability of the organization to achieve excellence will be hindered. Since the out-of-integrity manager will tend to find ways of removing those people who might have more knowledge or expertise than she does, the organization will be left without strong strategic competence.

If you work for an out-of-integrity leader, the likelihood is that you have often thought of leaving the job. I have seen two different approaches that seem to work with this type of leader:

1) More or less ignore the person. She realizes that she is out of integrity. Just give her the time to calm down. Let the emotions that she engenders just roll off your back.

2) Be kind and create a personal relationship. This is one of those situations where love may be able to conquer.

If you are a peer of an out-of-integrity leader, her emotional swings as she feels her lack of integrity, have probably affected you. The suggestions are pretty much the same as if you worked for this person (see above). But, especially if you are a peer, the second proposed solution will probably be effective. It might actually help her start the healing process.

What is good about this situation is that the out-of-integrity manager likely knows that she is out of integrity. If she works for you, then the following intervention may work:

- Personal therapy -- The person who is out of integrity needs to look inside and find a way to heal the issues with which she is not dealing.
- Leadership mentoring -- Once a leader has allowed herself to get into this style, it's difficult for her to see a way out of it. If she could see a way out of it she would've already done it. By acting out of integrity, she has created a suboptimal organization. Healing both organizational and interpersonal issues has some vastly complex components. Therefore when choosing a mentor for this leader, great care should be taken.

The mentor needed here is someone who has experience in leadership and psychology, and someone the person respects. The out-of-integrity leader needs someone who will not be bent to her will. Most consultants and coaches are swayed by their desire to maintain a long-term, financially beneficial, relationship. The mentor needs to understand that it is you, and not the out-of-integrity leader who is their boss.

Peer Leader

The peer leader is not someone who wants to lead their peers, but sees the people they lead as their peers. There seem to be two basic reasons why a person adopts this style:

1) She feels the loneliness of leadership and would rather have companions. Instead of looking to her hierarchical peers, she feels more comfortable looking to the group she is leading.
2) She has adopted the new age mantra that we are all special and that no one is special. This is true about the value of a person and her soul. We are not all the same when it comes to our jobs. The job of a leader is distinctly different from the job of a follower.
3) She has been temporarily appointed as a "manager" (manager in the NL sense), and will revert to being a peer at the end of the project. She doesn't know how to be a peer, then a leader, and then gracefully become a peer once more.

The peer leader can be recognized by how she interacts with her group outside of the work situation. If she swaps stories about her boss or other bosses with people in her group, then she probably has crossed the line from true leadership into the style of peer leader. The ability to compartmentalize is not a peer leader trait.

This leadership style works well when a group cannot see their leader as a real person. If they view her position with anything approaching awe, it can hamper the communication. This style can help lessen the automatic deference for hierarchical position that many people have. The overuse of this style results in a group that is unprepared for advancement. In addition, it is very difficult for a peer leader to give downside feedback.

If you work for a peer leader you may enjoy her, but miss the vision of a true leader. One of the issues with a peer leader is that she may think that which she values is the same as what her group values. As an example, I know one peer leader who structured her whole company around perks that she valued. Not everyone in her company valued those things. She was always surprised when they were angry with her. My suggestion is to talk with her and let her know what you value and what you want from your career. In addition let her know what type of leadership would help you excel.

If one of your peers is a peer leader, you may envy her the relationship she has with her group. But realize the cost. Helping her understand and accept the alone-ness of leadership can really help her grow into her position. Being alone is the separation from others in the group. This need not feel lonely.

If a peer leader works for you, she may give you many of the things you want and lack some of the things that are important. Future planning, employee reviews, and relaying hard decisions may all be difficult for her. Help her understand the role of the leader as providing goals and boundaries which help the group work better. By providing these supports, she may be more respected and better liked.

Narrative Leader

The Narrative Leader is not so much an individual style as it is someone who can pick and choose from a number of different styles, and uses them at the appropriate time and place. One of the distinguishing features is that she is able to verbalize the narratives of her group, individuals within the group, her boss, and the organization. With her understanding of these narratives, both foundational and expressed, she is able to form a leadership style that optimizes for the 3E's (see "3 E's," page 7).

The Narrative Leader is always searching for the optimum way of leading. You can recognize her style in that it is constantly in flux. For a few months she may have strong hints of one style and then add in other styles as the context changes. One way of recognizing a Narrative Leader is that if you ask her about how a person in her group operates she will be able to give you a brief narrative of that person.

If you work for a Narrative Leader, you can optimize your success by telling her what you need to excel. Don't try to bluff her with an ego-based narrative. Talk about your core narrative's version of success.

You may be able to learn a lot if you have a Narrative Leader as a peer. Listen to how she describes the world and watch how she reacts to new situations. Your reactions and analyses of the world may be different, but it's the process of how she views the world that is important.

As an employee, a Narrative Leader may be a handful to manage. She is always changing and adapting to context changes quickly. She may not be the most technically astute, or the fastest thinker, but she is the person that others will follow. In fact, others in your group may rather follow her than you. It can be difficult on the ego when your group looks to someone else for leadership. It is important to figure out a way to work together to lead the group. You have your position, and a good Narrative Leader understands the narrative of the hierarchy.

VII. Startups - The Beginning of It All

Start with the end in mind.

I've started several companies, been part of several other startups, and briefly worked in the venture capital industry. Founders are immensely excited by the potential of the product or service they want to bring out and are overloaded with the amount of work it takes to birth a company.

What I've seen is that in the chaos of creating products and processes from scratch, founders take shortcuts. "It's a hassle now, but it will be better later." "We don't have time to document it now, but we will catch up on that later." "This is the best person I know of, and we don't have the time or the money to search further."

There is no reason to stop taking shortcuts - until things fall apart. Shortcuts create an environment, a core narrative, that says "Shortcuts are okay" and "Stress is either to be ignored or relished" (i.e. stress = getting things done. More stress = getting more things done). The core narrative that is created is "People only matter if they help the gears of the organization spin faster." It creates an unhealthy environment, an unsustainable environment. No founder I've ever known set out to create a company that people dislike. But the vast majority of organizations are unhealthy work environments.

What the founders missed was that as soon as they became managers and executives, their jobs were no longer to bring out products or services, but to build an organization that worked well - one that emphasizes the 3E's (see page 11). All of the founders that I know, wanted a company that was an enjoyable environment, one that uplifted its people as well as made a profit. By concentrating on the profit and product/service, the founders lost sight of one of the basic reasons why they even thought of starting a company: they wanted a better place to work.

Over the years, I've followed many founders from starting their company through venture capital, and a few, through going public. The unfortunate thing I've seen is that the shortcuts that they took early on warped the organization and warped the founders.

A Short, True Story

Frank had been a mid-level manager with a large organization. He felt his career had topped out within the organization and that the people above him weren't making the best decisions. He gathered a few friends together and they founded a high-tech company. The hardware and software were all quite innovative. They put their life savings into building the first prototype. After two rounds of venture capital they had millions of dollars in orders and product started to flow out the door. Frank was a good man with a gentle heart and a sharp mind.

As the organization grew, financial pressures preceded cash flow by months to years. So Frank made decisions and shortcuts based upon the financial pressures. As you might imagine Frank's life became more and more stressful as he wandered further and further from the man he wanted to be. There came a point in time, just as the company was going public, when the financial pressures peaked. Frank made some decisions that were, at best, marginally legal. He knew that in a few weeks the situation would correct itself. Right then, he felt that he needed to show how strong the company was, so he made these decisions.

As Frank became less and less happy with himself it flowed out into the organization as a foundational narrative. The organization became less and less happy, a less healthy place to work.

A few months after the company went public, Frank had his first heart attack. Frank was a millionaire many times over. But like most of the millionaires I've known, he wasn't very happy. Frank didn't set out to be unhappy. He really wanted to build a company that was great to work for and made a nice profit. He lost track of the first part of his dream: creating an organization that he, and most of the people within it, really enjoyed working for.

Shortcuts don't scale.

If you plan on your organization growing, take the time to create the processes that aid in the growth.

The Narratives of Startups

There are a wide variety of reasons that people give for starting a new business. The exact reason is not as important as much as how it fits into the core narrative of the founder and what it is that you want to create.

When starting a new endeavor you are creating a foundational narrative for the organization. Over time the organization develops a foundational narrative separate from the founder. As it adds people and interacts with outside forces the foundational narrative develops its character. This is much the same as a new infant develops his own character as he grows through being a child, teenager, and adult.

For example, right now my company is pretty much a one-person affair. That's not to say I haven't had significant help from many others. I'm the developer of the majority of the technology, and for the moment, I'm the only one writing about it. Therefore, it might seem logical to assume that my foundational narrative is the same as the foundational narrative of my organization that encompasses Narrative Leadership.

One significant difference is that my foundational narrative ends with my demise, while I am designing the organization to outlive me. My foundational narrative has a distinct endpoint while Narrative Leadership's foundational narrative is much more open-ended. Therefore there are certain time related forces that may have me making certain decisions that aren't present in the foundational narrative of the organization. One way this plays out for the organization is that I am building structures and processes that will outlive me and that can easily survive without me (once these seeds are well planted, fertilized, and start to grow).

Another example: Years ago I consulted for a tea company. The owner's foundational narrative had a significant component that life is serious, business is serious, and business is hard work. He started a tea company because that was his passion and he found working with tea, drinking tea, and talking about tea, all as being deeply enjoyable (and almost fun). So although the individual foundational narrative was around seriousness, the organizational foundational narrative was around enjoyment. This came through very clearly in the organization's interactions with its marketing agents, suppliers, and customers. But when working with the founder it was all about serious work. This dichotomy created distress that prevented the organization from working as well as it might.

The two themes that I'm trying to illuminate here are:
1) When starting an organization look at that organization as separate from the founders. Therefore:
    - Logically and with forethought create an organization's foundational narrative.
2) Let the organization be separate, and in ways bigger than the founders. Those who limit their organization to meet only their own needs are greatly hampering the viability of the organization.

Passion & Narratives

There is an internal, expressed narrative that occurs when we start a business. We tell ourselves the stories of how we would like things to be and how we want them to be different from what we've experienced before. This internal, expressed narrative features our goals, our desires, and the narrative of why we are starting this business.

A good idea is not enough. It needs to be coupled with a passion for the mission of the company, and tied to a clear expressed and foundational narrative for the product/service of the company.

Startups are hard work. The normal bumps of leadership are hard enough, but in a startup it's combined with having no processes in place to handle the easy stuff (like where to put the copy paper), and for the harder stuff (like taxes and personnel policies). Not enough resources - so the founders have to seriously multitask. What has carried me through these darker times is my passion and the foundational narrative for the organization I'm trying to build.

When I talk about the foundational narrative of the organization, its a complete story of what I want the organization to be like, where it's going, why it's in existence, and how it exists separate from me but as part of me. I'll give you two quick examples from my consulting past.

One startup was a biomedical company founded by a brilliant engineer, Felicia. She had developed a new way of testing DNA samples. Felicia's foundational narrative was that she was an engineer. She saw the company building up around her which would allow her the time and resources to do further research and come out with amazing new products.

The second company was the tea company I mentioned before, founded by Fred. Fred had a passion for really good teas. He saw the company as an evangelizing agent for training American taste buds to prefer better tea.

Both of these companies became moderately successful in entirely different ways. They had expressed narratives that the founder could tell themselves and their friends. Their foundational narratives formed their companies in entirely different ways and placed the founder in entirely different positions (one as a researcher and the other as the prime PR agent for the company).

We keep ourselves going through hard times by reminding ourselves of our own narratives. Just as important is the ability to tell other people our narratives so that when hard times occur, our friends can remind us of who we are, where we're going, and why we are putting ourselves through this trauma.

Many of us, as teenagers, had the dream that we'd get a good idea, tell someone about it and they'd invest $1 million. Then, more or less, we'd have it made. As an adult we realize how much hard work is involved in creating anything: a healthy vibrant child or a healthy vibrant organization. What carries us through the hard times with our children is our love for them and the narrative we tell ourselves about how we want to be as parents. Similarly, what carries us through the hard times with our business is our passion and the narrative our support network feeds back to us.

Startups, Creativity, & Groupthink

When creating a new organization, substantial creativity is required to develop the processes, products/services, policies, and external relationships that the organization needs for the expression of its foundational narrative. Since there are no processes or policies in place, no one, including the founders, knows how to appropriately function. In order to prevent everyone from going off in their own direction, implicit boundaries must be set. These implicit boundaries help the organization focus on the most important questions. If the implicit boundaries continue into an organization's maturity, these boundaries can have a significant negative impact upon the organization's creativity. This focus, the implicit boundaries, is groupthink. In NL terms:

> **Groupthink**: *A systematic self-protection mechanism of controlling thought whereby an organization protects itself from questions that it doesn't want to answer.*

Groupthink is not bad or good, it just is, although, it may have good or bad consequences. Groupthink is the natural process by members of a group learning each other's way and the group's way (leaning the personal and organizational foundational narratives). Leaders need to be aware of the amount of groupthink that goes on and adjust their leadership style to optimize the group for the job at hand.

Startups are fragile things. Too many questions and the people and systems explode. Too few questions and the product or service doesn't match the market's needs. One of the many tasks of a Narrative Leader is to manage the delicate balance between too many questions and too little.

The balancing act starts with knowing your group. How well do they know the market? How well do they work with each other? And probably the most important question of all: How well do they handle open-ended questions – questions without definitive answers? When starting anything new there are a lot of unknowns and therefore a lot of open-ended questions.

Once the Narrative Leader has her initial feel for the group, the leadership task is to manage the ebb and flow – the protection from, and the inundation with – outside information. The more established the group and the closer the product or service is to completion, the more outside information is required.

When I have mentored startups, I try to be very gentle at the beginning. The goal is to help the founders steer a way through the rocky shoals of creating something new while holding steady on the guiding light of passion.

In my family of origin, we were trained to find the flaw in each other's thinking. This is a great way of learning how to think critically, but really puts a damper on the willingness to bring out something truly creative or new. Startups are like that. Lots of people can find the flaws, but if the goal is to bring out something new it takes a different mindset. It takes the willingness to stand back and allow the captain to steer. The challenge is to know when to say something and when just to support.

Continuing the oceangoing simile, it's like steering a supertanker versus sailing a catamaran. When we are by ourselves we are like a catamaran. We can change directions quickly. We can feel the wind. When we are leading a group, the speed with which we can change direction is much more slow. The group reacts to the winds of change and the waves of trials in a completely different fashion than a single person. Structuring the group so that it has the right amount of reactivity, creativity, and groupthink (self-protection) takes experience and thought. And it's not about getting it right. It's a dynamic balance.

It's a fragile time when we start a new venture. It's an elegant time. We should treat it as such.

Mission Statements & Knowing Who You Are

Some organizations try to approach knowing who they are with mission statements. In all my years of managing, consulting, and teaching, I have met only a handful of managers who could remember their organization's mission statement. In no case that I know of did the mission statement help an employee in her daily activities. Mission statements are not the same as a foundational narrative.

> **Mission statement**: *A carefully crafted expressed narrative whose general goal is to inspire rather than inform about the foundational narrative.*

Mission statements can be helpful, especially when dealing with investors. For some leaders, the act of developing a mission statement can help start them on the path to understanding the organization's foundational narrative. Forbes magazine suggests that mission statements should answer these four questions:
- What do we do?
- How do we do it?
- Whom do we do it for?
- What value are we bringing?

These are important questions. However, they don't answer the basic question that helps leaders on a daily basis: "How do I make decisions?" That is, what issues and values apply at this moment and in this situation.

This is not to say that mission statements are waste of time. They can be wonderful, good things that can help the select group that wrote them to understand the organization better. The caution is that, in general, the return on investment is not nearly as great as most consultants and management books would have you believe.

Catchphrases

Catchphrases are a great step towards understanding an organization's foundational narrative. Catchphrases have the advantage over mission statements in that they take significantly less time to develop and can more accurately portray various parts of the foundational narrative.

> **Catchphrase**: *A phrase or short sentence that is easy to remember and encapsulates a significant element of an organization's or individual's foundational narrative.*

For example, Google has an informal catchphrase of "Don't be evil." Narrative Leadership was started with the catchphrases: "Do the right thing" and "Creating an environment that works."

The first catchphrase is about our ethical approach to the world, business, and our employees. What "the right thing" is at any given time will be context related. It implies that ethics is the driver and that the context will be taken into account when making decisions. Ethics is primary. "The right thing" will become clear when the foundational narratives of the stakeholders are understood. This catchphrase states that we are an ethics driven company.

The second catchphrase is about the work that we do. We are trying to help create a society that contains jobs that people like, works well for the organization, and is of benefit to all stakeholders. The phrasing of this catchphrase is in the future progressive tense. That is, we are currently doing it and we will be doing it in the future.

Other catchphrases from major corporations include:
- GE – "Imagination at work."
- Amazon – "… And you're done."
- Ford – "Built for the road ahead."
- IBM – "We make IT happen."

- Lockheed–Martin – "We never forget who we're working for."
- Marylhurst University (where I teach) – "Dedication to excellence in the education of self-directed adult learners."

Some of these catchphrases could really help an employee understand how they are supposed to look at the world. Some of these catchphrases are just marketing gimmickry meant to make executives happy and consultants rich.

When discovering your organization's catchphrases, think about how you want the employees to frame their point of view: how do we view each other and how do we look at the world? Try to distill this expressed narrative into one short sentence. This is not about what you do, but about how you do it and what you value. Your catchphrases should embody both what you are today (the reality) and where you're going (the hope for the future). This catchphrase should embody a major issue in your foundational narrative. You might want to start the search by selecting one or more major topics within the foundational narrative (e.g. quick response, problem resolution rather than problem patching, healing the environment, etc.) The catchphrase should be short, to the point, a worldview, and helpful on a daily basis. It may take some time and effort, but it will repay itself many times over.

The phrasing and terminology used in the catchphrase is extremely important. It needs to reflect clearly and cleanly a significant element within the foundational narrative. It also needs to be memorable. Sometimes clarity and memorability conflict.

Sometimes catchphrases come easily and quickly. Sometimes they are are a long and arduous labor of love. You'll know when they're right because you and others can easily remember them, they help you make difficult decisions and, when you tell it to someone new, they get the point of the foundational narrative that you were trying to illuminate.

Hiring for Startups and Young

Organizations

There are many pitfalls for a young company trying to find, hire, and retain good employees. As previously stated, most founders think that their organization will be better/different from where they worked before. The problem with this way of thinking is that it is a reaction to something (usually bad), rather than striving for something great. It's like a teenager who doesn't want to be like her parents. By being in reaction to their way of being. she either turns out very much like her parents or she ends up creating a new set of problems at the opposite extreme. She feels like she has two choices: 1) be just like her parents or 2) be nothing like her parents. She doesn't realize that there are a wide universe of other choices.

In terms of hiring for startup organizations, there are vast array of choices for hiring processes and methods of compensation. For example, most high-tech startups give nearly the same pay as larger organizations but offer significant stock options to offset the many uncertainties and the large workload. For the average initial employees, the stock option is just a chimera. He either leaves the company or the company goes under before the stock option has any real value. Even for those organizations that survive, the majority of stock options produce relatively small rewards. As an example:

In 1981 I started a company that came out with the first scanners for the PC market. We had 5 million shares of stock, and the average employee received between 5000 and 50,000 shares as stock options, in line with other high tech companies of the time. As the company grew we had to go through multiple rounds of financing. At each round of financing, the new investors required us to issue more stock to give to them. After three years the company had issued about 50 million shares. This gave our early employees between 0.01% and 0.1% each of the total stock (on average just enough money for a very nice family vacation). It is very rare that early employees become millionaires, even in very successful companies.

Your organization does not have to be like everyone else's. However, if you do opt for something different, there will need to be an education of the potential new employees. When looking at compensation packages, start by looking at the organization's foundational narrative. What does the organization's foundational narrative have to say about the following issues and their relationship to compensation:

- How much say do employees have in the direction of the organization?
- What is expected of the employees?
- What qualities are required of potential employees? E.g. self driven, highly creative, focused, playful, take direction well, future oriented, etc.

Startup organizations are prone to doing things fast and dirty. There are few resources, and all the leaders are multitasking. The hiring process works within this stressed environment and is further hampered by most leaders' dislike of the hiring process. This creates a high likelihood for taking shortcuts in finding and hiring the top candidates.

For example, at one startup I was with, the hiring process was that Human Resources (one person) would bring me a pack of résumés that she thought filled the requirements for a job opening in my group. There was enough money in the budget to have one or two of the candidates fly in for interviews. If none of the résumés in the pack filled my group's needs, I'd have to wait a few months before Human Resources had time to collect more résumés. For expediency's sake, most managers would just select the best candidate that was in the first pack of résumés.

Another problem was that when we wrote the job description, there was no place on the form for personality type, communication ability, or other important group interaction facets of their character. All of us were hard-pressed for time. So we probably appreciated that we didn't have to think about those things. But of course, that came back to bite us as the company grew. What we had were many dysfunctional groups and many people doing ego-based politics. Within a few years, the company had become a deathly place to work.

The easy route for staffing a young organization is to hire friends and acquaintances. This has the advantage of speed, hiring a known quantity, and that your friends may be the best in the world for your startup. The disadvantages include harming friendships, and potentially staffing with less than the excellence you want from your startup.

A more difficult but standard practice is to collect résumés and interview the people with the best résumés. This standard practice has the advantage of being a known and well-used process with a large pool of candidates. The disadvantage is that the best employees are not looking for work.

A third alternative is to make a list of the attributes of a dream candidate and a second list of the top people, worldwide, that have these attributes. Find out all you can about these people: what might their foundational narratives be? Then create a plan for approaching these people, and do it. They may say "No," but many of them will suggest someone that they think may even be better. Who knows, they may say "Yes." Think of how this great hire may help your organization blossom. Early hires have a tremendous affect upon the future of your endeavor. This method has the advantage of finding employees that can give your organization a tremendous strategic advantage. The disadvantages to this method are that it can be scary to approach these top candidates and it may take more resources than the other approaches.

Each of these methods of staffing has their advantages and disadvantages. There are three methods of staffing listed here, there may be many more alternatives.

Begin the way you want to continue.

The first hires will help form a significant part of the core narrative for your startup. If you don't mind your core narrative being haphazardly flung together, then you can hire pretty much anyone. If you care about creating an organization that is truly different and better than the ones you have been in before, this is going to require significant time and attention to the hiring process.

The people hired, and the integration of these people into the organization makes a huge difference.

> *In complex systems the beginning state has a significant determination upon the end state.*

VIII. Selecting a Team

The prior section, ""Hiring for Startups and Young Organizations," page 144, concentrated on the startup issues around hiring of the first few employees. This section deals with the overall selection process, regardless of the organizational maturity.

Frequently, a leader only gets to select a few of their team, the rest are already in place. The steps listed here can help when the team is fully staffed, partially staffed, or with no current staff.

Five Step Hiring Process

The first step is to determine what characteristics you want as the core narrative for the group (see the section ""Foundational Narratives," page 44 for more information on core narratives). This is not about the technical aspects and the techniques that the group might use to solve problems (e.g. cooking, programming, bricklaying). This step is about deciding on the essence of how the group will think about itself and how it will make decisions.

For example, I once formed a new quality assurance group for a high-tech firm. Although my budget would not allow me to hire very senior people, I wanted the group to think of itself as very experienced, professional, and wise in the ways of handling touchy professionals. With this core narrative in mind, I was then able to do step two.

Step two is to determine some ways in which this core narrative would express itself in people's résumés, work history, interviews, recommendations, and where these people might be working now. For example, if I were going to add an employee to my current company I'd be looking for someone who felt that her mission in life is to help the world be a better, more caring, more creative place. This might express itself in her résumé by her selection of companies that she worked for, that she probably didn't stay very long at any one company, that she was constantly educating herself, and that she chose creative oriented positions. In the interview process she would show vitality mixed with respect, grace, desire, and creativity. The recommendations might not come from the her boss and at least some of them would be from her coworkers. When I called the people who wrote the recommendations they'd comment about how much they missed her and how she loved to solve problems in ways that benefited all concerned. I would look for this special person in small communication oriented companies, self employed in the communication/people relations area, or possibly displaced mathematicians or psychologists working in creative companies.

Step three is to look at the people you have in place: yourself and any existing members of the group. For example:
- How do their foundational narratives play together?
- Where do their foundational narratives help each other be excellent and where do they get the group in trouble?
- What is already excellent amongst this interplay?
- What aspects could use some help?
- What expressed narratives are tending towards destruction?

Understanding problem areas helps to determine where your leadership talents will be challenged. Understanding what is good helps to determine the areas that need to be protected and encouraged, i.e. preservative leadership.

Preservative leadership*: When a Narrative Leader works to maintain the best parts of the interplay of the narratives of the group.*

Step four is looking for the one or two people who exemplify the core narrative. Most managers might start by hiring the person with the most technical experience, the person who will be the lead. That's great if this person also exemplifies the core narrative. The first person hired sets the precedent for the group. If the first hire does not exemplify the core narrative, it makes it much harder for the group to ever develop the core narrative at which you are driving. Remember, start the way you want to continue.

Step five is filling out the group in a way that grows the group's core narrative, person by person, ever closer to the desired narrative. As each person is added to the group, the Narrative Leader adapts her criteria for the group and hiring into the group. This is a part of enhancement leadership.

Enhancement leadership: *When a Narrative Leader modifies her leadership style in order to enhance the 3E's of the group and of each member of the group.*

When selecting new people, the selection criteria for the next person to be hired is modified by each previous hire. For example, suppose I were trying to staff an engineering group that would design the next great high-tech tool. My selection criteria would include: 1) out-of-the-box thinking 2) broad knowledge of similar tools already on the market 3) knowledge of a broad area of manufacturing techniques and capabilities 4) deep knowledge of how people use similar tools and what they like and don't like about those tools, and 5) a firm understanding of how this organization works and decides, and its current capabilities.

Let's say that the first person I bring into the group has been with the company for many years and completely fulfills criterion number five. My future hires need to fulfill criteria number one through four. My second hire is a young engineer who fulfills the criteria number one and four. My final hire must fulfill criteria number two and three. As each person was added to the group I changed my major criteria for the next hire. This constant adaptation of the decision criteria is a component of enhancement leadership.

Finally, step six is analyzing what your leadership narrative needs to be in order to round out the group and help it move towards the desired core narrative. This is the major component of enhancement leadership. For me, step six has been the most difficult to figure out and implement. We all come to leadership with some preconceived notion of who we are and what it means to be a leader. Step six is about stepping back from this and looking at the situation from a totally new vantage point, one separate from these preconceived notions. This is a monumental task. It is hard to know when you are seeing the world objectively or through your own rose-colored glasses. Friends and mentors can be of great assistance. Once you understand what your role needs to be, stepping into that role fully can also, initially, be a difficult task. It's a step out of your comfort zone and into a different expressed narrative. Remember, leadership is the art of creating an expressed narrative that helps people excel.

I have heard some managers state that the way they manage is a clear expression of who they are, i.e. modifying how they lead people would not be true to themselves. Enhancement leadership is not about being untrue to oneself. All of us express ourselves in a variety of ways, all of which are true to who we are. We express ourselves differently to friends and enemies, acquaintances and family, on the Internet and in person, etc. Most of the time we subconsciously choose what what we say and how we are going to say it, depending upon the audience. Enhancement leadership asks us to bring this into our consciousness and to extend our communication ability so that we produce the 3E's in those we lead while being true to ourselves.

To recap, the six steps:
1) Determine a desired core narrative for the group.
2) Hypothesize how this core narrative might show itself in expressed narratives.
3) Analyze the interplay of foundational narratives of the current group. What works well and what doesn't?
4) Identify the one or two people who most clearly express the desired core narrative.
5) Add these people to the group, one at a time. Each step should move the group closer to the desired core narrative. Adapt the criteria for further hires as each person is added.

6) Determine an optimal leadership narrative that assists the group in fulfilling the group's core narrative and aids each person in their move towards excellence.

Creating an Environment That Works

FAIRNESS, EQUALITY, AND NARRATIVES

We have three basic ways of understanding the world and our foundational narrative. These are the ways that we've been taught since birth: auditory (through sound, speech, and music), visual (through our eyes or when we visualize something, e.g. art, photographs, charts, and maps), and kinesthetic (through touch and the sense of our bodies, e.g. dance, athletics, and learning by doing). We live out our foundational narrative through these modes of understanding and communication.

For example, part of my foundational narrative is around writing. The narrative revolves around joy, clarity, inspiration, and awe. These are kinesthetic aspects of my foundational narrative in that I feel them in my body. For example, for me there is a specific feel to clarity - I feel it as an ease that permeates my torso and arms. There are also auditory and visual aspects of the writing part of my foundational narrative - I like to talk out my writing. It helps me think more clearly. Therefore, I use dictation software so that I can just talk (auditory) what I want to write. Then, I like to print out what has been written and edit on the printed page, because, I like the look of it (visual). Looking at my writing when it's done pleases me (a kinesthetic emotion) and reinforces the kinesthetic reasons for why I write.

Now let's look at how to lead someone like me. If I was my leader and I wanted to increase the productivity and creativity of my writing, I would look at what gets in the way of (my foundational narrative around) my writing and what assists it.

What gets in the way:
- A messy desk (not enough room for all my research materials and to move around).

- Noisy environment (hampers the voice recognition software).

What assists:
- A good monitor and printer so that I can see and enjoy the final product.
- A good voice recognition system so that I can speak out my thoughts and move around while I'm writing.

Being my own manager and making sure I have these things is simple. Too often, though, I've seen organizations that have a foundational narrative of treating everybody equally and translating that into an expressed narrative that everybody gets the same things.

As an example, I use a voice input for most of my computer tasks. Most of my friends use a keyboard. If our leader was to go out and buy the best computer keyboards, the most ergonomic, the best tactile feel, then most of my friends would feel valued. But I would feel discounted. The same perk for all of us resulted in two very different effects.

As leaders, it is our job to understand what motivates the people we lead and what gets in their way. It's not an easy job. Most often it's a messy job. Real life and real people are awe-inspiringly complex.

Where most leaders make a mistake is that treating people fairly is not about our way of looking at fairness but the receiver's way of looking at fairness. That is, a Narrative Leader must have some understanding of the foundational narrative around fairness, of the people they lead. The fallback position for leaders is to treat people equally, which can be very unfair.

Treating people equally is not necessarily fair. Treating people fairly is not necessarily treating people equally.

ENTRANCES & EXITS

Searching for a new job is a major life stressor. Beginning the job can be exciting, but is also quite stressful. As leaders, why do we pay so little attention to the stress state of our new employees? In addition, when a new person enters a group, the entire group's narratives are forced to change. This is especially true since the person entering is in a stressed state. My experience is that leaders tend to ignore the individual and group stresses and act as if it's business as usual, i.e. "People don't really matter, only the tasks do."

On the other end of employment life is when people leave, the group dynamic also changes. Most frequently when someone leaves there is little explanation as to why, and no understanding of the stress the leaving creates upon the group and its remaining members.

Each new beginning creates a pattern for how things will continue. Each new ending reverberates, recalling all the previous endings and deaths that the person and group have experienced. We bring people in and assist them to leave. We treat people as interchangeable resources.

Each time someone enters or leaves, the group stresses accumulate. Stresses are amplified when someone leaves quickly and without comment, such as when someone is fired. When we ignore these stresses, we ignore the humanness of the people we work with. We are treating individuals as interchangeable, replaceable resources, something to be used while it's necessary and tossed away when the work is done. "He," "she," "you," and "me" become "human capital." We have not only neutered others and ourselves, we have de-vivified everyone. We choose to treat each other as inanimate and unfeeling objects. This is one of the reasons why I hate the title of the group "Human Resources." This title exemplifies that we treat people exactly like capital resources, computer resources, paper clips, and pens.

There is another way. All we need do is to treat the situation as the reality that it is: each person feels, has dreams, and has a life outside of work. We are much more than the tasks that we do for our employer.

Many organizations have rules for managers about what they can say and what they cannot say when a person leaves. Most of the time, these rules are interpreted to mean, "Say nothing!" But, even in the most restrictive organization, a leader could bring his group together and discuss how each one feels about the situation and the recent departure. As a Narrative Leader, these acts of understanding can greatly change the stress level. Even showing that you are trying to understand the stress can help significantly to reduce the overall stress level. Once you have an understanding for the stress level and how it's being handled you, as the leader, can start to devise a strategy and expressed narrative to handle the issues.

A Narrative Leader has many options on how to handle the entrance of a new person into a group. A good start is to show the new person that you will treat them as a human, with emotions and with talents. Find out how stressed they are and how they think about themselves as they enter this new job. Show them that you, too, are human and that the group is a human assembly.

I've seen managers introduce a new hire at a meeting. Each group member introduced himself, and then the meeting went on with its normal business. There is no "getting to know you" chatter. A new cog in the wheel has been inducted into the system.

A better way to introduce the new hire might be to have a meet-and-greet lunch or coffee. Let people mill around and act like real human beings. Give people time to tell their stories to the new hire. This beginning allows the new hire to enter the group's narrative in a more natural fashion.

> *Stress, swept under the carpet, brings organizational dis-ease. Stress well handled brings organization robustness.*

HIRING & DYNAMIC TENSION

> **Dynamic tension**: *The stress created when two or more people get together and they don't think exactly alike. It is caused by the differences in personality styles, backgrounds, learning and communication styles, level of self-knowledge, and general approach to life.*

Dynamic tension can be thought of as being similar to a choir singing. Each person's voice is an expression of his thoughts. When two voices are in perfect harmony there is no dissonance. This takes significant skill and talent. If the singing voices are off, even a little, the disharmony can be heard. Similarly, if two people's thoughts differ from each other, as they normally do, there exists a dynamic tension, despite, or because of, the skills and talents of these individuals. Therefore, in any group there will be dynamic tension, sometimes this can be quite significant. The more dissimilar the expressed narratives are within the group, the higher the dynamic tension. Dynamic tension does not have to be destructive. One of the reasons groups are sometimes so effective is that within the group there are many minds approaching problems from many viewpoints. Too much tension, though, can significantly reduce creativity and efficiency.

Before hiring anyone I pause for a while and think about the amount of dynamic tension that I want and can handle. This becomes part of my hiring criteria. It's easiest to hire someone who thinks exactly as we do, or as close as we can find. It's comfortable. It's also not dynamic. Unlike a choir, perfect harmony doesn't move towards creativity or change of any sort. When I consider hiring, I gauge the level of creativity that I want to bring into the group:

- How much additional stress can the group handle?
- How much additional stress can I handle?
- How important is it to inject creativity into the group?
- How much does this group presently do groupthink?

I ponder on this before writing the description of the perfect fit for the position. This "perfect fit description" describes the personality and the narratives of the human that I want for the position. This is not a "job description" it is a "human description." Having this human description helps me write the job description, and augments it significantly. Since I rarely advertise for jobs, this writing helps me determine who I'm going to talk to about these openings and how I'm going to language the opening. When I've had to work with large human resource departments, this information has helped me train the HR people in searching for the right fit.

Determining the right amount of dynamic tension is based upon the art of knowing your team. Many managers know the projects, know the company, know the corporate goals but don't know their team well enough to understand the level of stress that they are under. Too little stress and the group begins to die (Retired-In-Place). Too much stress and the group will fracture. Up to a point, stress can drive creativity, but over that point creativity drops very quickly. Also, not enough stress and people don't feel challenged - they will start looking for new jobs. Too much stress and people will sabotage projects and look for new jobs.

Start the task of evaluating the dynamic stress within your group by talking to your peers. Get their input on what they think the current level of dynamic stress is within your group. As the leader of the group, you live inside the stress, so it is much harder for you to see and feel it objectively. Ask lots of people, some of whom may only know of your group tangentially. Then, make your own analysis. If you have a mentor or consultant you trust, talk over your tentative analysis with her. Realize that this is a learning process, a new skill for you. It may take many trials, but each time you re-analyze the situation, you will probably be a little more accurate.

There is no perfect balance within a group – it's dynamic, always moving through the balance point to an unbalanced point and back again.

IX. Metrics

In a 2013 survey of CEOs, over two thirds said they were frustrated by the lack of meaningful measures of the organization's performance. Almost half felt that they didn't have a good handle on their executive team's performance. In addition, over one third had been "blind-sided by a negative surprise in the last 90 days." ["What Keeps CEOs up at Night?" Kapta LLC]. The use of metrics can significantly ease and enhance a leader's understanding of their group's foundational narrative. Metrics can increase performance and decrease surprises.

Types of Metrics

Metric: *A direct or indirect measure of a foundational or expressed narrative.*

Direct metric: *A measure of a person's or group's expressed or foundational narrative.*

Indirect metric: *A measure of a <u>leader's understanding</u> of a person's or group's expressed or foundational narrative.*

If an organization does the same thing over and over again, and never innovates, managers could make schedules that achieve organizational goals almost all the time. But rarely do we make a schedule to do something that we've already done before. Usually we are innovating. Therefore there are unknowns and possibly some uncontrollable unknowns.

Schedules are a retrospective metric: "Did we make the schedule, or did we miss it?" Many leaders try to estimate the present level of completion and compare that to the amount of time that has elapse. The idea is, "If we have completed x% of the work and are x% of the way through the schedule, then we are right on schedule." This only works when the work load is linear. That is, the first day's work requires the same level of creativity as the last day's work and every other day in between. Rarely is this true. The leader can try to overcome some of this problem by making the schedule more fine grained, but the data it gives is still retrospective data.

Good metrics can greatly aid a leader's ability to achieve the 3E's within her group. Currently, there are almost no metrics that will tell an executive how well their leaders are actually leading their groups. This is different from whether the group is achieving its goals. I've known many managers who were miserable leaders, but their group continued to achieve its goals. The group overcame the leader's shortcomings.

Executives tend to rely upon made or missed deadlines, the organization's bottom-line, and how easy or difficult they are to manage. None of these are real measures of how good a leader the person is. Some of the best leaders miss deadlines for reasons that had nothing to do with their leadership ability. It happens.

Metrics can be divided into three groups based upon what the time orientation of the information is:

Retrospective metric: *A measure of past events that tell how well things went in the past.*

Current metric: *A measure of past or current events that informs how well things are going in real, or near-real, time.*

Prospective metric: *A measure of past or current events that informs how well things may go in the future.*

Most metrics in use today are retrospective. For example, the quarterly earnings report isn't really telling anything about the present or future. As discussed in prior sections the bottom-line measures management's decisions made many months and possibly many years ago.

One of the main areas of emphasis in Narrative Leadership is the move towards metrics that are current or prospective. Narrative Leadership aids in assuring the quality of managers and leaders. In order to do so there must be measures and definitions of what is leadership quality. To date, I have developed over 15 metrics that measure various aspects of leadership quality. Within this chapter are listed three metrics that are the most fundamental and easiest to utilize and understand. For information on other metrics, see the website at www.NarrativeLead.com.

Measuring Foundational Narratives (Surprises)

WHAT IS MEASURED

Surprises measure a leader's understanding of the foundational narratives of his group, his peers, the organization, and external forces. The results of this metric can be used to guide a leader in focusing on the areas that are most likely to give future problems. Therefore, this is considered a prospective metric.

HOW SURPRISES WORKS

If a leader perfectly understood all of the foundational narratives affecting the current situation, she would never be surprised. Since she understands how everybody makes decisions, she knows how each person will react to an issue, therefore, no surprises. For example, if Marcia perfectly understood how her family and friends felt and thought about her and her birthday, they could never spring a surprise party on her. Marcia would know in advance if and when it was coming. She would pick up the little signs that give away the secret.

We are surprised because we cannot perfectly understand our own foundational narrative much less anyone else's. This is what allows us to be surprised. If Marcia keeps track of her surprises, she would see who, where, when, and how her understanding of foundational narratives is lacking.

Some readers might question if the surprises are supposed to be organizational surprises, surprises that can be agreed upon by a group, or surprises that the leader herself experiences. The answer is that this metric measures the leader's understanding of the foundational narratives. Therefore, any time the leader is surprised she should mark it down.

Explanation & Example

Keeping track of surprises can be as simple, or as complex, as a leader wants to make it. For example, every time Marcia is surprised she could jot it down on a sticky note, and then put it on her wall. Every few weeks she could review the notes and see if a pattern emerges. A slightly more complex alternative method is to use the worksheet in the appendix: ""Surprises & Sparks Worksheet," page 177".

The Surprises & Sparks Worksheet is meant for use during meetings. Whenever a surprise occurs, a corresponding mark is placed on the chart. For major or more interesting surprises, notations can be made as shown in "Figure 6: Surprises & Sparks Example." Information that might be collected include:

- Description of the surprise.
- The size of the surprise (small, medium, or large).
- Where the surprise came from:
    - Internal to your group.
    - External to your group but within the organization.
    - External to the organization.
- Who informed you about the surprise?
- Hierarchical level of the author giving the surprise:
    - A peer.
    - Someone lower on the hierarchy scale.
    - Someone higher on the hierarchy scale.

Marcia can use this information to determine where she needs to focus her attention and what she needs to learn more about. Most managers spend their educational time learning more about the technology or industry in which they manage. That is, they become better and better at things they already know well. This metric helps leaders to focus on things that they don't know as well.

Most major problems occur in areas where the leader is not looking. If Marcia had paid attention to the surprise area, she could have avoided or lessened the problem. Again:

What we pay attention to, determines what we miss.

An example worksheet is shown below. Note that this worksheet combines the tracking of surprises and sparks, the next metric to be discussed.

```
Meeting: SilverTime exec committee      Date: 7/16/2012
Start Time: 10:00
End Time:   1:00
```

! Surprise ★ Spark

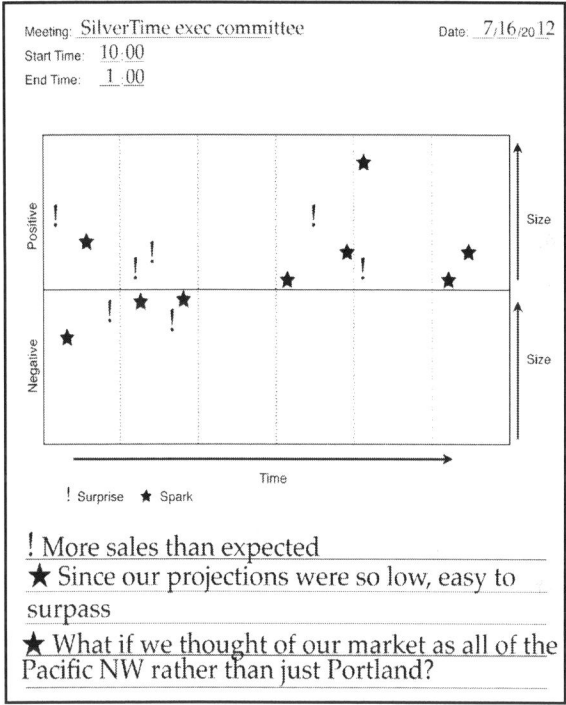

! More sales than expected
★ Since our projections were so low, easy to surpass
★ What if we thought of our market as all of the Pacific NW rather than just Portland?

Figure 6: Surprises & Sparks Example

The tracking of surprises can be extremely useful for annual personnel reviews. Surprises can be used as both a measure of how an individual performed in the past, as well as being used as a current metric. For example, over the past year Edward has given many surprises by withholding information (and therefore waiting for things to get really bad before surprising his leader with a really big surprise). At the next annual review Marcia, his manager, lets him know specifics about his past behavior and gives him guidelines for future behavior. Edward gave 50 big surprises by withholding information this past year. The goal is to change his behavior so that he gives a maximum of one big surprise per year from withholding information. Having no surprises would be nice, but changing behavior takes time. Surprises are tracked and information fed back to Edward on a monthly basis. Edward averaged 4.7 surprises per month over the past year (although his worst month was December with 8 surprises). This year's goal is no more than 4 surprises per month for the first quarter, 3 surprises per month for the second quarter, 2 surprises the third quarter, and 1 for the fourth quarter.

Marcia and Edward both track the surprises. At regular intervals they discuss the differences in their tracking of surprises. One of the advantages of this method is that it helps both parties understand each other's foundational narrative. This is especially helpful when the surprises have been large, indicating a significant lack of understanding.

Measuring The Work Environment for Innovation (Sparks)

Creating an environment that balances innovation with stability is very difficult. Innovation allows the organization to evolve, rather than devolve. Stability allows the organization to plan for the future and manage its resources to achieve specified goals. The challenge for a leader is directing this innovation while maintaining good working relationships between groups and between employees.

Most of the time, innovation comes in tiny, incremental steps. Things like using staples rather than paperclips because they're less expensive. In my experience, groups have hundreds of small innovations per week. Most of these little sparks of creativity are forgotten almost immediately. These uncaptured innovations add up. In a typical midsize company, approximately 10,000,000 innovations are lost every year. Some of these might have been small, in fact the majority probably were. But these small innovations, if implemented can become a significant strategic advantage. The larger, but uncaptured, innovations may have become major new products or services. It is too easy to loose these sparks of innovation amidst the chaos of everyday life.

When an organization optimizes itself for small innovations, large ones are likely to be optimized too. That is, when people feel encouraged to innovate, the part of their mind that is creative is given more energy and attention.

Sparks are a current and prospective metric. That is, sparks inform a leader about the current environment for innovation, and if no major changes occur, they predict the environment for future innovation.

What is Measured

A spark is anything that feels like an innovation or change. Sometimes I may track the size of a spark: big spark, midsize spark, or small spark. This allows me a feeling of freedom to record the smallest spark of innovation along with big creative thoughts.

This metric measures each individual's spark of innovation. That is, this is not a leader's view of the state of innovation. Sparks are each person's own new ideas. Attention to sparks helps the organization capture these small innovations and to consciously decide what they want to do about it. In addition, leaders can watch the ebb and flow of these sparks. When a leader understands what decisions increase or decrease these sparks, he can then adjust his expressed narrative of leadership to optimize innovation.

Note that sparks are not only positive ideas about how things might be better. Sparks include downside ideas too, like: "The strength of that plastic won't hold the given load." Properly managed, these downside sparks could save an organization a lot of time, money, and frustration.

How Sparks Work

I generally ask each person in my group to track their own sparks. Whenever they feel even a small spark of innovation they jot it down and share selected ones later. This metric also works, though not quite as effectively, if only the leader is tracking sparks.

In general, I jot down a short description of the spark and when the spark occurred. This allows me to track sparks against changes in the environment (e.g. major decisions, personnel changes, or schedule changes).

EXPLANATION & EXAMPLE

When I am in a meeting, I track sparks and surprises together on the same sheet. See the worksheet in the previous section for an example. The basic idea behind spark tracking is that when we measure a behavior we can optimize the environment to enhance or limit that behavior.

Unmeasured behavior is uncontrolled behavior.

Adaptation to the chaotic world environment can be either controlled or uncontrolled. Controlled is better.

For example, let's say Melvin leads a customer service group. He would like his group to innovate new ways of supporting the customers as well as lowering the cost of support. The typical way that Melvin could handle this is to have a brainstorming meeting. If his group has been well trained to switch into the brainstorming mode of thinking, this may work well. The greater problem is that brainstorming is an occasional, at best, practice. Much innovation is lost in between brainstorming sessions.

Melvin is a smart Narrative Leader. He tells his group about sparks and asks them to track their sparks and share their best thoughts. Every month he gives a $25 gift certificate to the person who has shared the most sparks that have been adopted by at least two other people in the group. A $50 gift certificate is awarded to anyone who has had a spark adopted at the company level. He awards these gift certificates at a monthly "Sparks Pizza Luncheon." Thus everybody in the group is rewarded for participating, and there's a little something extra for good ideas.

Measuring Implicit Leadership (Golden Glow)

As discussed in the earlier section "Explicit & Implicit Leadership," page 27, implicit leadership comes from a group wanting to follow a given person. The implicit leader has developed an expertise, a personality trait, or a trained ability that draws people in. I call this skill the "Golden Glow" because it is a warm reflection upon an elegant leader.

If you have been appointed to your position, how do you know if you also have an implicit leadership authority as well as a hierarchical authority? This metric will help you determine how much of an implicit leader you are.

The Golden Glow is a prospective metric in that it informs a leader as to how well people may follow her in the future (if there are only small changes from the present). Golden Glow measures followers' willingness to open themselves up to being led by this leader.

What is Measured

The Golden Glow is a measure of respect for a leader. It is designed to show how much the narratives of others describes you as a leader.

Level of respect for a leader: *The amount of overlap between a follower's foundational narrative regarding what constitutes a leader and the expressed leadership narrative of a leader. That is, how well a leader matches a follower's ideal.*

The level of respect can vary greatly depending upon the overlap of foundational narratives:
- No overlap - No respect.
- Slight overlap - Grudging respect.
- Moderate overlap - Some respect as an implicit leader.
- Significant overlap - Great respect as an implicit leader.

The level of respect can be judged by the four types of questions that people can ask you as a leader:
1) They ask a question that they think you **know** the answer to, and is **related** to your area of expertise as a leader.
    - Example: You are a software engineering manager. A group member asks you a programming question.

2) They ask a question that they think you **know** the answer to and is **unrelated** to your area of expertise as a leader.
    - Example: You are a software engineering manager with a new car. A group member asks you about new cars.

3) They ask a question that they think you **do not know** the answer to but is **related** to your area of expertise as a leader.
    - Example: You are a software engineering manager and new to the company. A group member asks you what software tools are available within the company.

4) They ask a question that they think you **do not know** the answer to, and is **unrelated** to your area of expertise as a leader.
    - Example: You are a software engineering manager. A group member asks you what grunge bands are playing in town this week.

To some extent, whenever someone comes to you and asks a question, they are showing a level of respect for you as an implicit leader. The type of question determines how much of this respect is being shown. The least level of respect for you as an implicit leader is shown in question type #1. Each question type shows more respect than the previous type.

Golden Glow: *When a leader is asked a question that the questioner thinks the leader **does not know** the answer to, and is **unrelated** to the leader's area of expertise in their job. A Golden Glow question is a display of the highest measure of respect for a leader.*

How often do people come to you with a Golden Glow type of questions? For a question to be a true "Golden Glow," your part of the interaction must be a non-self-interested transfer of data. An example of a "self-interested transfer of data" is what's commonly called gossip. There are multiple purposes to gossip. One of them is to build up a pseudo-leadership role. It's not a real leadership role, in Narrative Leadership terms. Gossip's purpose is neither to guide the other person to be a better person nor to assist the organization in working better. One of the main purposes of gossip is to build a relationship to the advantage of the gossiper. Nothing is inherently wrong with building a relationship, it's just that in this context it is not building implicit leadership. Gossip creates pseudo-leadership.

Pseudo-leadership: *Where the purpose of leading is for the gain of the leader rather than the gain of the people being led.*

How Golden Glow Works

There are two parts to this. First is trust. If people come to you with questions that they figure you don't have a ready answer for, then they are coming to you out of trust in you as a leader. This is a huge deal. If you are unsure whether or not someone approached you from the viewpoint of your not knowing the answer, you can ask them. This doesn't show your lack of knowledge; it shows your interest in them and their question. For example, Melvin could ask, "Why are you asking? Do you think I might have a ready answer?"

The second part of this metric is "Are you a leader of a pseudo-leader?" If you skew your answer to the person's question in order to build the relationship, then this doesn't count towards the Golden Glow. Not that working on the relationship is bad. It's good.

The point is that when you're working on the relationship, or your ego, or any other of a number of issues, it lessens the positive impact of the interaction upon your implicit leadership. Either you are using the question to build yourself up, or you are keeping the question pristine - which then builds your implicit leadership.

If you're still unsure as to whether or not the person thought that you knew the answer, you can either count it or count it as a half.

EXPLANATION & EXAMPLE

This metric can be especially useful if you're relatively new to a group, have been recently promoted, or are a consultant. In any case, an essential part of being a Narrative Leaders is taking an annual review of how effective you are as leader.

An example of the use of this metric: I once had a manager who thought of himself as a great manager. Max the Magnificent Manager was, in my opinion, pretty awful as a leader. So I suggested to him that he try a modified form of this metric. I asked him to track all four types of questions. Being the magnificent manager he was, he must get lots of great questions. I left it up to him to do his own analysis. Within two weeks he stopped referring to himself as so great a manager. There were some changes, but I understand that within two years he had left the ranks of management. Max was too stuck in his way of leading and he he didn't want to change.

If you are an executive or second level manager, this metric can be helpful when you are training others to become leaders. As the trainee analyzes the questions she gets, she can begin to understand how people see her. This can be a gentle way of getting people to look at their affect upon others.

X. What's Next?

If you choose to pursue Narrative Leadership, the next step is to start implementing NL in your life. The easiest way to start is by choosing one of the metrics and start using it.

Why Start With Metrics?

1) The metrics are designed as a window into other people's foundational narratives. They can act as focal points for introspection and discussion.
2) Metrics are easy. They are designed for easy data collection. Once you get used to the data collection it will take only seconds to log each data point.
3) The metrics are designed to be viruses. There are two parts to this.
   - Firstly, once you start gathering the data, it has an effect upon your thinking. You will naturally start acting more like a Narrative Leader.
   - Secondly, in general, data wins. If one person in an organization starts demonstrating hard data about innovation or what management needs to be focusing upon, then they will probably win arguments against those who have hand-waving impressions and slick PowerPoint slides of potential futures. Hard data wins! As one leader starts to win arguments with hard data, some of the other leaders will look into these metrics and Narrative Leadership.

After you have begun collecting data, start verbalizing your understanding of NL. Talk with your friends and peers about your initial impressions regarding Narrative Leadership and your initial understanding of other people's and organization's narratives. Go to the NL website and enter into the discussions. Find a mentor and discuss your findings. Verbalizing helps clarify thinking.

Start by looking at expressed narratives, rather than foundational narratives. They're much easier to see. Expressed narratives point towards the underlying foundational narrative. If you spot certain issues that you think are part of the foundational narrative, keep track of them. But, especially don't get hung up on trying to differentiate different parts of the foundational narrative yet. Keep it simple initially. You can always add complexity, but if you get lost in the complexity it can be difficult to regain the simplicity.

There are many more tools to aid a leader in discovering foundational narratives. Three that I would like to suggest that take more in-depth training then this introductory book can give:

- Neurolinguistics – This is the study of how our words (linguistics) effect our thinking (neurology) and conversely how are neurology effects our communication. This is a large area of study and is best done in-person rather than through book learning alone. The reason for this is that much of our communication is nonverbal. It is difficult to learn nonverbal communication skills through verbal/visual means like a book.
- Narrative therapy and narrative psychology – These are the study of how our stories have an effect upon our ability to interact socially. Michael White and David Epston started this area of inquiry. They've written several books on narrative therapy. One of their best books is an out of print book titled "Literate Means to Therapeutic Ends." There are also many other good authors in this genre.
- Learning styles theory – This is the study of how people understand their world and communicate with other people. Many authors have taken the basics and applied them to specific areas. In fact neurolinguistic programming (NLP) has incorporated this as a major part of its approach.

Follow up with mentors, classes, and questions. Expand your knowledge. Look at where you have been surprised. Focus on increasing your knowledge in those areas. If NL feels surprising to you, there's assistance through the website:

www.NarrativeLead.com

In brief, here are the steps:
1) Select one of the metrics and start using it in its most basic form.
2) Discuss what you're finding.
3) Find people and resources to help you grow as a leader.

May your way be filled with great stories and your life be filled with peace and joy.

Fond regards,
Rabbi Rob
April 2014

XI. Appendices

Mental Health Resources

Mayo Clinic - If you know what you're looking for, this site has a good deal of information. This is a good secondary site to add more details to your knowledge base.

http://www.mayoclinic.com/health/mental-illness/DS01104

The Mayo Clinic has a great webpage for information about narcissism. This may help deepen your understanding of the narcissistic leader:

http://www.mayoclinic.com/health/narcissistic-personality-disorder/DS00652/DSECTION=symptoms

Mental Health America - This site is designed for someone who has a mental health issue. It's a good resource for those with such a challenge and who want to excel at work.

http://www.mentalhealthamerica.net/go/finding-your-balance-at-work-and-home

National Institute of Mental Health - A great deal of information is hidden throughout this site. The site is oriented around medical research, but there is a vast store of information for the lay person. A good place to start investigating this site is:

http://www.nimh.nih.gov/health/publications/the-numbers-count-mental-disorders-in-america/index.shtml

US Department of Health and Human Services - A truly excellent site for Narrative Leaders to understand mental health issues.

http://www.mentalhealth.gov/

WebMD - This website has some good information. The information it does give is accurate, but banal. It's information-lite. This is a good solid place to give yourself a one minute overview.

http://www.webmd.com/mental-health/default.htm

Wikipedia - I've learned not to fully trust the information from Wikipedia. For professional leaders it's great for giving an overview and suggesting resources. Try and stick to scholarly material and not information by or for laypeople. There's a tremendous amount of quackery on the Internet.

https://en.wikipedia.org/wiki/Mental_health

https://en.wikipedia.org/wiki/Mental_Illness#Prevention

World Health Organization - There are a wide variety of resources available through the WHO. The first site listed is about work and mental health. The second one is their general mental health site.

http://www.who.int/mental_health/media/en/712.pdf

http://www.who.int/topics/mental_health/en/

APPENDICES 177

Surprises & Sparks Worksheet

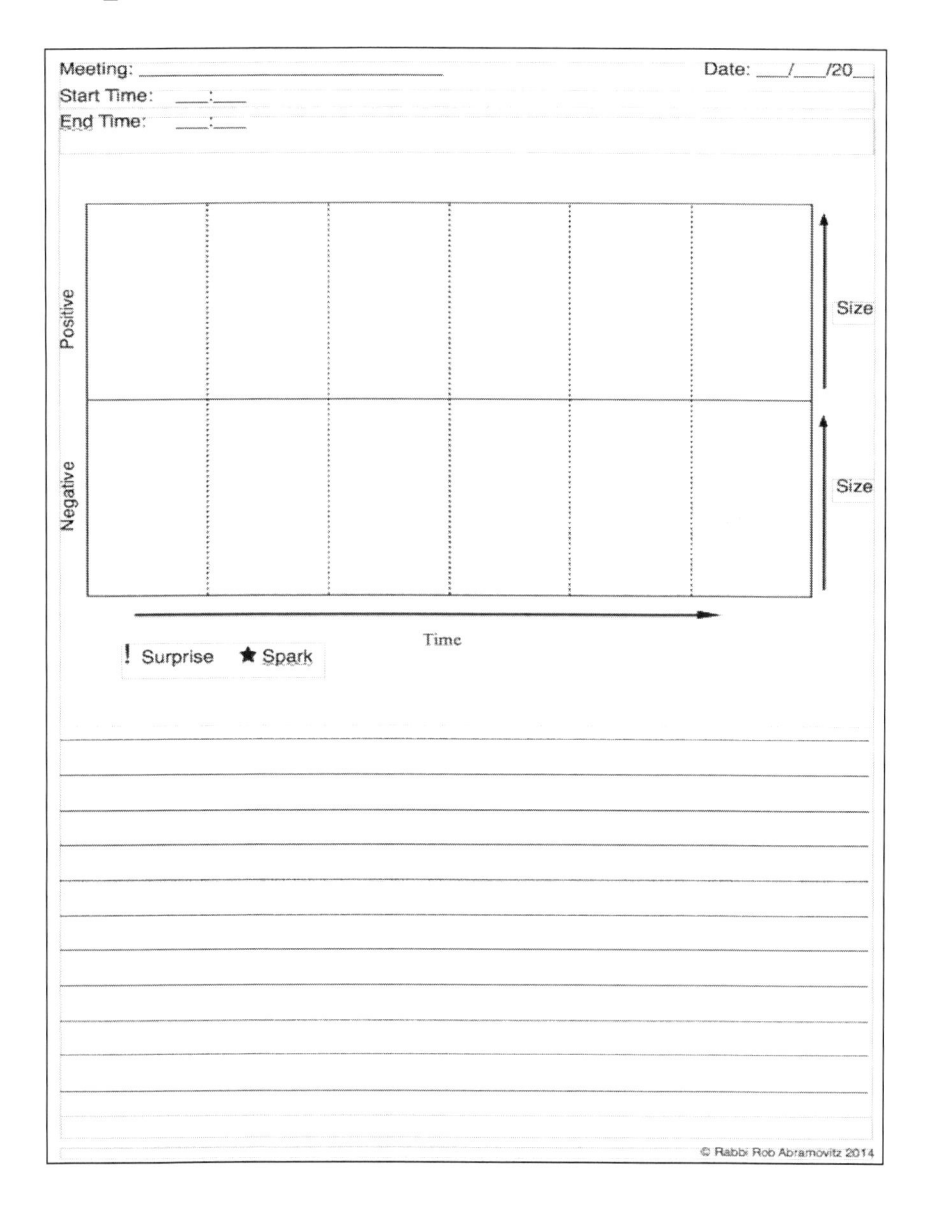

Meeting: _____ Date: ___/___/20___
Start Time: ___:___
End Time: ___:___

Positive / Negative vs. Time — Size

! Surprise   ★ Spark

© Rabbi Rob Abramovitz 2014

Worksheet notepads can be inexpensively purchased through our website, **www.NarrativeLead.com.**

Glossary

3 E's: Elegance, Efficiency, and Efficacy.

Adaptive narrative: The part of a foundational narrative that changes with the environment, i.e. context sensitive. (See "Foundational narrative" and "Core narrative.")

Assumptive words: A shortcut verbalization from the foundational narrative though the expressed narrative that show biases and attitudes that the speaker does not expressly state. A type of shorthand.

C-suite: The executives of an organization. So called because most of the members have "C" for "Chief" in their title (e.g. Chief Executive Officer, Chief Technology Officer, etc.).

Catchphrase: A phrase or short sentence that is easy to remember and encapsulates a significant element of an organization's or individual's foundational narrative.

Clear narrative: An expressed narrative that is a clear expression of the underlying foundational narrative. (See "Narrative.")

Code word: A word or phrase used by a subculture or cult that has a distinctly different meaning for the subculture than for the larger culture. The purpose of these code words is to differentiate the subculture from the overlying culture and/or to assist the subculture in hiding out in plain sight. (See "Communication level: Dialectical.")

Communication level: The hierarchy embedded into communication:

Up: Deference. For example: "You might think of it this way" versus "Think of it this way."

Down: Superiority. Examples abound: ordering someone to do something rather than asking, snobbery, aloofness, and refusing to answer questions.

Even: Peer. The language tends towards the informal. More frequently a back and forth discussion rather than a monologue.

Dialectical: In opposition to. Examples include: Us/Them, code words (see "Code words"), and technical jargon. Technical jargon might include RAM (computer memory), toroid (a bagel shape), atherosclerosis (hardening of the arteries), and acronyms of all sorts

Core narrative: The part of a foundational narrative that is slow to change or changes only with major life events. (See "Foundational narrative" and "Adaptive narrative.")

Current metric: A measure of past or current events that informs how well things are going in real, or near-real, time. (See "Metric," "Prospective metric," and "Retrospective metric.")

Diamond ethic: A structural ethic that has been tested multiple times and under great stress against other structural ethics. The diamond ethic is the one(s) that is consistently more valued. (See "Ethics," "Structural ethics," and "Good idea ethics.").

Direct metric: A measure of a person's or group's expressed or foundational narrative. (See "Metric" and "Indirect metric.")

Direct trust: Granting of trust because the person giving the trust has a personal understanding of the foundational narrative of the person or organization being trusted. (See "Trust" and "Referred trust.")

Diversion narrative: An expressed narrative crafted to divert others from searching further. (See "Expressed narrative.")

Donut hole manager: A person who struggles to get ahead in order to fill an unrecognized hole in the foundational narrative. For this person there is never enough, until he recognizes the lack for what it is. (See "Manager.")

Dynamic tension: The stress created when two or more people get together and they don't think exactly alike. It is caused by the differences in personality styles, backgrounds, learning and communication styles, level of self-knowledge, and general approach to life.

Efficacy: Produces the desired results with few, if any, undesirable side effects. One of the 3E's. (See "3E's," "Efficiency," and "Elegance.")

Efficiency: No unnecessary distractions. One of the 3E's. (See "3E's," "Efficacy," and "Elegance.")

Ego-based politics: The interplay of narratives where the outcome for one group or individual comes at the expense of the organization, other groups, or other individuals without their willing consent. (See "Politics" and "Operational politics.")

Elegance: An optimal and intuitively appropriate fit to the need. (See "3E's," "Efficiency," and "Efficacy.")

Enhancement leadership: When a Narrative Leader modifies her leadership style in order to enhance the 3E's of the group and of each member of the group. (See "Leadership," "Leadership narrative," and "Preservative leadership.")

Ethics: A part of the foundational narrative to which the person or organization ascribes value. (See "Diamond ethic" and "Good idea ethic.")

Excellence: A talent or quality that is unusually good and so surpasses ordinary standards. Also used as a standard of performance.

Explicit Leaders: Leaders who are appointed by a hierarchy. (See also "Implicit leaders" and "Leadership narrative.")

Expressed narrative: The truth as we tell it to others and how we want them to believe. (See "Foundational narrative.")

Foundational narrative: The truth the individual or organization (as narrator) believes in, and upon which she makes decisions. (See "Expressed narrative.")

Golden Glow: When a leader is asked a question that the questioner thinks the leader *does not know* the answer to, and is *unrelated* to the leader's area of expertise in their job. A Golden Glow question is a display of the highest measure of respect for a leader. (See "Implicit leaders.")

Good idea ethic: A part of the foundational narrative whose value varies depending upon the context. (See "Ethics," "Structural ethics," and "Diamond ethic.")

Groupthink: is a systematic self-protection mechanism of controlling thought whereby an organization protects itself from questions that it doesn't want to answer.

Image narrative: An expressed narrative crafted to show the person or organization in a certain light. This is the majority of expressed narratives.

Implicit Leaders: Leaders who arise from a consensus of the people she leads. (See "Explicit leaders" and "Leadership narrative.")

Indirect metric: A measure of a leader's understanding of a person's or group's expressed or foundational narrative. (See "Metrics" and "Direct metric.")

Issue Storm: "Swirling, turbulent flows of information that blow up when people try to deal with complex issues. Our world is increasingly dominated by issue storms. Our lives are issue driven and chaotic. Our interaction with others is complex and unpredictable" [D. Wojick, "Chaos Management And the Dynamics of Information: a New Way to Manage People In Action:(Especially During Paradigm Shifts)"].

Leader: A person who guides people towards specific goals, such as excellence at her job, good communication, and understanding how she fits into the bigger picture.

Leadership narrative: Creating a story that works for all of the stakeholders. (See "Leadership narrative, alternate definition" and "User narrative.")

Leadership narrative (alternative definition): The purpose of leading is to enable others to excel within the group framework. (See "Leadership narrative" and "User narrative.")

Lean manufacturing: The process of inspecting each part of an organization and evaluating which tasks and subtasks create value for the customer, where there might be waste, and taking steps to eliminate the waste.

Level of respect for a leader: The amount of overlap between a follower's foundational narrative regarding what constitutes a leader and the expressed leadership narrative of a leader. That is, how well a leader matches a follower's ideal.

Management gestalt: The entirety of what it takes to be a good manager. The form and substance of a manager. "Gestalt" is from the German, meaning "form" or "shape."

Manager: A person who conducts the business affairs or operations of a group or organization. (See "Leader.")

Managing-up: The art of handling those above you in the hierarchy such that it makes your life easier or better, or makes your work more efficient and effective.

Meme: An idea that spreads from person to person, much like a virus. Meme's are single ideas that may combine to form a meme complex. (See "Meme complex.")

Meme complex: A set of closely inter-related memes that join to create something larger than each of the memes separately. (See "Meme.")

Menschlichkeit: The art of being a graceful human being.

Metric: A direct or indirect measure of a foundational or expressed narrative. (See "Indirect metric" and "Direct metric.")

Mission statement: A carefully crafted expressed narrative whose general goal is to inspire rather than inform about the foundational narrative.

Narrative Leadership (NL): A model for guiding organizations and people towards excellence by the directed use of story.

Narrative: A story that contains elements of the past and present, has a projection of possible futures, and the narrator is central to the storyline.

Negative trust: Where there is an understanding of another person's, or an organization's, foundational narrative and it violates the principle or ethic inherent in your own foundational narrative. (See "Trust" and "Positive trust.")

Nucleus: The part of the expressed narrative that contains the clear expression of the foundational narrative. Frequently the most significant part of the nucleus is the desire for power. (See "Expressed narrative," "Spin," and "Overlay.")

Objective reality: A massively shared view of the world that answers the relevant questions that individuals and organizations ask. That is, a self-consistent narrative that operates within an open universe of questions. (See "Subjective reality.")

Operational politics: The normal give and take of the interplay of narratives where the outcome is positive for the organization and no group or individual is significantly negatively impacted without their consent. (See "Politics" and "Ego based politics.")

Overlay: The part of the expressed narrative that contains what looks like objective truth. (See "Expressed narrative," "Spin," and "Nucleus.")

Peter Principle: Managers choose a person who is the best at one job and promote him to the next higher job. Slowly, he will become competent at the new job, and then start to excel again. He gets promoted again and again, until he finally hit his base level of incompetence.

Politics: The interplay of the narratives of the various participants. (See "Operational politics" and "Ego based politics.")

Positive trust: Where there is both an understanding of another person's, or an organization's, foundational narrative and it overlaps with your own. (See "Trust" and "Negative trust.")

Preservative leadership: When a Narrative Leader works to maintain the best parts of the interplay of the narratives of the group.

Prospective metric: A measure of past or current events that informs how well things may go in the future. (See "Metric," "Current metric," and "Retrospective metric.")

Pseudo-leadership: Where the purpose of leading is for the gain of the leader rather than the gain of the people being led.

Referred trust: Granting of trust because of the person or organization that is the intermediary is trusted. (See "Direct trust" and "Trust.")

Respect: A person's regard for a person or organization whose foundational narrative strives towards a higher purpose.

Retired-in-place (RIP): Someone who has reached a place of comfort, and is unwilling to continue to learn and advance.

Retrospective metric: A measure of past events that tell how well things went in the past. (See "Metrics," "Current Metric," and "Prospective metric.")

Self-leadership: The art of looking inward for ways to increase elegance, efficiency, and efficacy (the 3E's), and doing something about it.

Shark: A person who attacks as part of their foundational narrative. The attack is not cause related or context related, but related to the stories that are going on internal to the individual.

Spin: The part of the expressed narrative that moves the narrative from the overlay towards the desired goal of the foundational narrative. (See "Expressed narrative," "Nucleus," and "Overlay.")

Stakeholder: Any entity that has an interest in the organization. This includes employees, shareholders, the community in which the organization resides, and regulating bodies.

Story: The telling of an incident or a series of events. The telling can be oral, written, or even just thought about. (See "Narrative.")

Storyline: A detailed description of the plot.

Structural ethic: A part of the foundational narrative to which value is ascribed and, around which the individual or organization has structured their thinking process. (See "Ethics," "Good idea ethics," and "Diamond ethic.").

Subjective reality: A view of the world that answers the questions the individual or organization is willing to ask. That is, a relatively self-consistent narrative that operates within a self defined universe. (See "Objective reality.")

Teachable moment: A relatively short period of time where an individual's or an organization's foundational narrative is undergoing a structural change and is open to outside suggestions. This usually occurs after a shock to the system. In more aware individuals this can occur when they feel that their current foundational narrative won't get them to where they want to be.

Technology: In Narrative Leadership terms, a structured process for modifying foundational narratives.

Trust: Understanding the foundational narrative of another person or organization. (See "Direct trust" and "Referred trust.")

Tuned feedback: Data about the state of a system that is easy to gather, intuitive, timely, and pinpoints critical needs.

Unit of control: The method or tool that a leader uses to control the speed, direction, and interactions of the group.

L:E&D

Leadership: Education & Development

Printed in Great Britain
by Amazon